# A STUDENT GUIDE TO RESEARCH
# IN SOCIAL SCIENCE

S

# A STUDENT GUIDE TO RESEARCH IN SOCIAL SCIENCE

**Renate Howe and Ros Lewis**
Centre for Australian Studies
Deakin University

CAMBRIDGE
UNIVERSITY PRESS

Published by the Press Syndicate of the University of Cambridge
The Pitt Building, Trumpington Street, Cambridge CB2 IRP, UK
40 West 20th Street, New York, NY 10011–4211, USA
10 Stamford Road, Oakleigh, Melbourne 3166, Australia

© Cambridge University Press 1993
First published 1993

Printed in Hong Kong by Colorcraft

National Library of Australia cataloguing in publication data
Howe, Renate, 1939 – .
A student guide to research in social science.
Bibliography.
Includes index.
ISBN 0 521 40888 1.
1. Social sciences – Research – Methodology – Handbooks, manuals, etc.
2. Library orientation – Handbooks, manuals, etc. 3. Report writing –
Handbooks, manuals, etc. I. Lewis, Ros, 1948– . II. Deakin University.
Centre for Australian Studies. III. Title.
300.72

Library of Congress cataloguing in publication data
Howe, Renate.
A student guide to research in social science / Renate Howe and Ros Lewis.
Includes bibliographical references and index.
Summary: A step–by–step guide on how to undertake research which investigates
various aspects of society using surveys, interviews, biographical research,
and other methods.
ISBN 0–521–40888–1
1. Social sciences—Methodology.  2. Social sciences—Research.
[1. Social sciences—Research. 2. Research.]  I. Lewis, Ros, 1948– .  II. Title.
H61.H77  1993                                        92–39527
300' .72—dc20                                        CIP
                                                     AC

A catalogue record for this book is available from the British Library
ISBN  0 521 40888 1  paperback

# CONTENTS

List of figures . . . . . . . . . . . . . . . . . . . . . . . . . . . . . . . . . . . . . . . . 6
Preface . . . . . . . . . . . . . . . . . . . . . . . . . . . . . . . . . . . . . . . . . . . . . . 7
To the student . . . . . . . . . . . . . . . . . . . . . . . . . . . . . . . . . . . . . . . . . 8
Acknowledgements . . . . . . . . . . . . . . . . . . . . . . . . . . . . . . . . . . . . . . 9
1 Planning your research project . . . . . . . . . . . . . . . . . . . . . . . 11
2 How to find and use existing resources . . . . . . . . . . . . . . . . . . 19
    Using a library . . . . . . . . . . . . . . . . . . . . . . . . . . . . . . . . . . . 19
    How to use books and articles . . . . . . . . . . . . . . . . . . . . . . . . 27
    Newspapers and the electronic media . . . . . . . . . . . . . . . . . . 34
    Community . . . . . . . . . . . . . . . . . . . . . . . . . . . . . . . . . . . . . 50
3 Doing your own research . . . . . . . . . . . . . . . . . . . . . . . . . . . . 57
    Surveys . . . . . . . . . . . . . . . . . . . . . . . . . . . . . . . . . . . . . . . . 58
    Using computers for your research project . . . . . . . . . . . . . . 68
    Interviews and oral history . . . . . . . . . . . . . . . . . . . . . . . . . 71
    Participant observation . . . . . . . . . . . . . . . . . . . . . . . . . . . . 86
    Material culture and visual resources . . . . . . . . . . . . . . . . . . 90
4 Putting your research project together . . . . . . . . . . . . . . . . . . 105
5 Annotated bibliography . . . . . . . . . . . . . . . . . . . . . . . . . . . . 111
6 Glossary of terms . . . . . . . . . . . . . . . . . . . . . . . . . . . . . . . . 117
7 Index . . . . . . . . . . . . . . . . . . . . . . . . . . . . . . . . . . . . . . . . . 121

# List of figures

*Figure*   *Title*                                                                      *Page*

**Chapter 1. Planning your research project**
1.1      Flow chart of steps in a research project ......................... 10
1.2      Steps in a research project ...................................... 11
1.3      Step 1: Choosing a research topic ............................... 13
1.4      Step 2: Your aim and research questions ......................... 14
1.5      Sources of information .......................................... 15
1.6      Step 3: Sources of information .................................. 16

**Chapter 2. How to find and use existing resources**
2.1      Deakin University library plan .................................. 21
2.2      Audio-visual microfiche ......................................... 23
2.3      Microfiche and microfilm readers ............................... 24
2.4      The anatomy of an academic book ................................ 30
2.5      The anatomy of a periodical ..................................... 31
2.6      How to use statistics in graphic form ........................... 35
2.7      Types of newspapers ............................................. 36
2.8      What's in a newspaper? .......................................... 38
2.9      Storing and indexing news clippings ............................. 40
2.10     Analysis of a newspaper front page .............................. 42
2.11     Tabulation of content analysis .................................. 44
2.12     Use of graphics ................................................. 45
2.13     Letter-writing .................................................. 54

**Chapter 3. Doing your own research**
3.1      Classification questions ........................................ 61
3.2      The 1991 Census was an enormous survey .......................... 62-3
3.3      Computer hardware and software .................................. 69
3.4      Interview record ................................................ 75
3.5      Informant profile ............................................... 76-8
3.6      Participant observation session ................................. 88
3.7      Evaluation of meeting participation ............................. 89
3.8      Comparing house plans identifies family relationships .......... 91
3.9      'Face to face' shopping before World War II ..................... 92
3.10     The changing streetscape of Victoria Street, North Melbourne ... 93
3.11     Street survey — data collection form — social and architectural ....... 94
3.12     Street survey — data collection form — environmental ............ 96
3.13     Artefacts data sheet ............................................ 99
3.14     Crocheted doily ................................................. 101
3.15     Family history .................................................. 102
3.16     Pictorial data sheet ............................................ 103

# PREFACE

Most Australian schools now require the completion of a research project as a major component of assessment in the inter-disciplinary humanities and social science courses recently introduced into the senior year curricula. As with the discipline-based courses, the ability to undertake independent research and to write a thoughtful analysis is regarded as a measure of student achievement at the secondary level.

It is important that the inter-disciplinary research projects develop a high level of research skills, as for many students they will replace history or geography subjects that had a strong emphasis on research methodology. The emphasis on developing research skills is more difficult in the inter-disciplinary subjects as the methodology they draw on is of necessity more eclectic. The task of developing research skills, given the vast range in the preparation and ability of students as well as the range in school research resources, is considerably more complex than with discipline-related courses. This complexity is compounded by the diffuse subject matter studied by students in preparation for the project. Compared with undertaking a research project related to Renaissance history, students of inter-disciplinary subjects may not have followed such a prescriptive course.

Despite these complexities, it is important that a focus on achieving substantial and well-conducted projects is maintained and that students graduate from the secondary school with credible research skills. It is one of the most important skills that students take with them into the future, contributing not only to their ability to understand and evaluate issues that affect them personally, but also, even in a small way, to an understanding of the society in which they live.

This is a practical book. It introduces the student to a number of research tools, guides them to existing information, and provides them with ways of collecting data that will make their work accessible and appropriate to be written up and presented as a final report. It is also a book about research on Australian society, and it encourages students to reflect the complexity of the Australian experience in their research and to be aware of the contribution of their projects to the broader society of which they are a part.

# TO THE STUDENT

If you are in Year 11 or 12 at an Australian secondary school and studying a humanities or social science course, you will need to carry out at least one enquiry or piece of individual research. To complete a really good research project, you need skills, help with finding resources, and guidance for the preparation and presentation of your project.

In the area of skills, we introduce you to a range of research methods you can use for your enquiry. We have placed considerable emphasis on research as a systematic business that needs careful planning and preparation. For this reason, we have designed a number of forms for you to photocopy which will help you in planning your project and recording the results of your investigations.

You will be able to use this book at all stages of your research project. Use it by choosing the parts which are most relevant to you; you won't need to use all of it. It is also an introductory book. If you are interested in following through a particular research skill, you will need to consult other books. We have included an annotated bibliography to help you do this.

Remember, research is not a mystery. If words or ideas are introduced that you may not understand, they are explained the first time, and included in a glossary at the back of this book.

Research takes planning and time, but it is a very satisfying part of your school studies, helping to develop useful skills and understanding about the world you live in.

Renate Howe and Ros Lewis

# ACKNOWLEDGEMENTS

Many members of the Centre for Australian Studies at Deakin University have contributed to this book. Chair, Peter Hocking, has given support and advice; Dr Shurlee Swain wrote the section on oral history; Dr Fazal Rizvi gave advice on participant observation, and Ruth Lee contributed to the section on material culture. The faculty of Humanities support staff, Judy Waldie and Val Lestrange, saw through the preparation of the manuscript with care and interest.

Our daughters, Sarah and Samantha, provided practical advice on the problems and advantages of secondary school research.

Renate Howe
Ros Lewis

Figure 1.1　Flow chart of steps in a research project

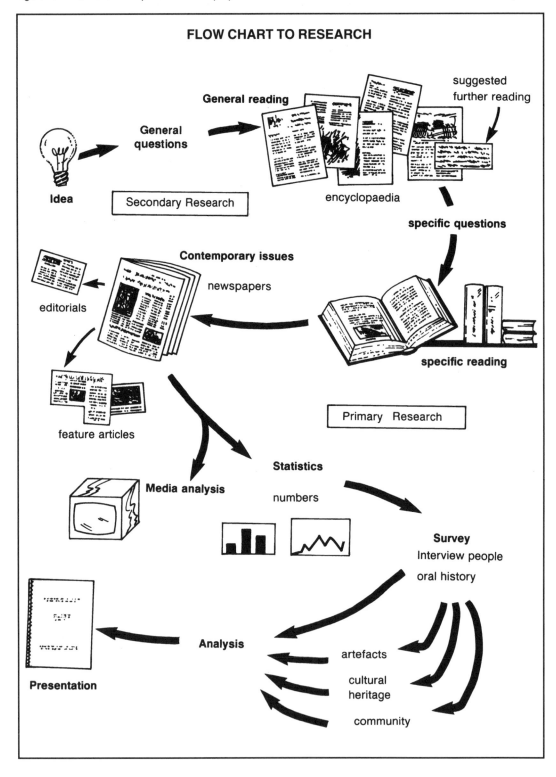

**FLOW CHART TO RESEARCH**

General reading

General
questions

suggested
further reading

**Idea**

Secondary Research

encyclopaedia

specific questions

Contemporary issues

newspapers

editorials

specific reading

feature articles

Primary　Research

**Statistics**

numbers

Media analysis

Survey
Interview people
oral history

Analysis

artefacts

cultural
heritage

Presentation

community

# PLANNING YOUR RESEARCH PROJECT

Careful planning of your research proposal will make your research easier and the final preparation of your project a dream rather than a nightmare. A research project is different from writing an essay or doing a maths exercise in that you will need to take more care in planning your time and work strategy.

All this work and planning will make more sense if you are convinced of the importance of the work you are about to do, so remember that a properly conducted research project will:

* develop skills which will not only be useful in later studies but in your every-day life;

**Steps in a research project from a general idea to writing up.**

General idea
▼
Background reading
▼
Refine topic and develop research questions
▼
Do more specific reading and research
▼
Define the research proposal
▼
Identify sources of information
▼
Develop appropriate research strategy
▼
Do research
▼
Analyse data
▼
Write up your project

Figure 1.2   Steps in a research project

- add to your own and other people's knowledge about the society in which you live. Even the smallest research project can contribute to a more meaningful understanding of Australian society.

Planning a research project is easier if you do it in steps. We suggest four planning steps and have included proposal forms for you to fill out and hand to your teacher for each of these steps.

# Step 1: Choosing a research topic

Your research will be easier if you choose a topic you are interested in. Don't be swayed by your friends, or do the same topic as the rest of the class. An issue that you would like to explore and which builds on other studies you have done will be a big advantage. If you are uninterested in your topic the work will be a chore and this will show through in your final report.

Your area of interest should fit in with the overall themes of your course. In each Australian state, research projects are related to courses with different themes and purposes. Your topic should give you the opportunity to follow through in depth the broad themes of the course you are studying.

Once you have decided on a general topic, your next task would be to undertake some background reading in this area, using the resources in your school and local library. (Refer to Chapter 2, Using a library.)

# Step 2: Your aim and research questions

This is the most important part of your project, and it is worth giving it some long periods of thought. Your background reading and your own interests are likely to have raised possible research topics.

But a research project is not just an exploration of some interesting questions. Nor is it a descriptive account of an interesting group or person or event. It must analyse people in society; it must *ask* and *answer* questions.

*At the heart of a research project is a hypothesis to test.*

At the heart of a research project is a *hypothesis* or idea that you want to test. Your research must have an aim, and you must be able to draw some valid conclusions at the end.

It is often difficult to sum up your research aim in a single sentence or short paragraph; after all, this is the heart of your project. However, even complex research proposals are often reduced to a short statement of aims in applications for funding, so you, also, should be able to produce a brief statement of the purpose of your research enquiry. It is a good exercise, then, to set out clearly and in a few sentences what you are setting out to research.

It is also helpful to follow up the statement of your aim with some related research questions. This will help you to set priorities in your research strategy. Follow this up with more focused reading that will help you develop your research proposal.

Figure 1.3   Step 1: Choosing a research topic

## Step 1: Choosing a research topic

Area of interest: _____

_____

_____

_____

_____

Explain how your area of interest fits in with the overall themes of the course:

_____

_____

_____

_____

_____

_____

_____

List at least four books containing background reading related to your topic that will help you define your research questions.

_____

_____

_____

_____

_____

_____

**Present to your teacher or research team for approval.**

Figure 1.4  Step 2: Your aim and research questions

## Step 2: Your aim and research questions

Provide a brief statement of the aim of your research project

_____

_____

_____

_____

_____

List some related research questions which your project will focus on.

_____

_____

_____

_____

_____

_____

Name some specific books related to your aim and research questions

_____

_____

_____

_____

_____

_____

**Present to your teacher or research team for approval.**

Figure 1.5  Sources of information

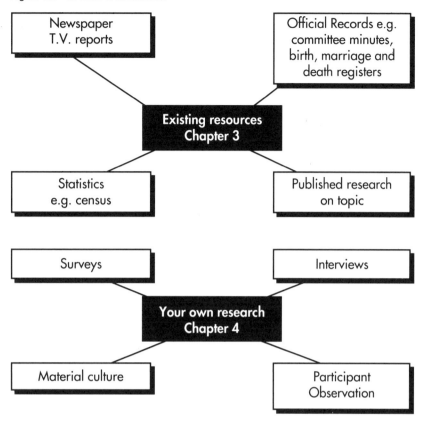

# Step 3: Sources of information

Most of this book is a guide to the relevant sources of information and the methodologies you will need to gather material for your project.

Begin by identifying the most easily available resources such as census material or newspaper files. Make sure that you can gain easy access to these resources; don't start out on a marvellous research project that you don't have the resources to undertake. Country students should keep in mind that they have more restricted access to data than city students. (See Figure 1.5: Sources of information (Existing resources).

The next step is to decide on the original research or first-hand information that you will gain through surveys, oral history or the other methodologies discussed in this book.

The sources of information you choose will be determined by your
• topic,
• access to information, and
• resources.

Figure 1.6   Step 3: Sources of information

## Step 3: Sources of information

**Existing sources**
List existing data bases such as census material or newspapers relevant to your
research topic.

_____

_____

_____

_____

_____

_____

_____

_____

**Original research**
Specify which of the research tools you will use, e.g. survey, oral history, etc. Give details of
the number and type of interviews etc.

_____

_____

_____

_____

_____

_____

_____

Attach copies of questionnaires, letters seeking information or other relevant information
**Present to your teacher or research team for approval.**

Most of you will use two or more methods of research for your project. For example:

| Topic | Methodologies |
| --- | --- |
| Print Media and Women's Sport | • Analysis of newspaper content.<br>• Interview with people involved, e.g. sports writers, athletes, team managers.<br>• Questionnaire survey of participants. |
| Changing Nature of Women's Domestic Work | • Statistics.<br>• Participant observation.<br>• Oral history interviews.<br>• Material culture analysis, e.g. needlework. |

These are suggestions only. Be selective and make sure you have the most appropriate sources for your topic. Don't try to use too many methodologies.

## Step 4: Planning your research strategy

How can you get everything done in time? It is important to work out a timetable early on to make sure that your research tasks are manageable. You will need to be specific here, as there is a lot of 'hidden' time in research (arranging interviews, phone calls, thank-you notes) that you should take into account.

*This is the time to go to Chapter 3 of this book which tells you about types of research and how to do them.*

The stages of this process provide for feedback from your teacher and/or research team if appropriate; you can amend and modify your proposal as you find out more about your subject and the realities of undertaking research. Remember, no-one, not even the most experienced researcher, produces a well-thought-out proposal first off. All proposals benefit from consideration, advice and adjustment.

Finally, write a paragraph on what you expect to be your research outcomes — a very useful paragraph for you to come back to as your research proceeds. Indeed, at this planning stage, it would be useful to refer to Chapter 4: Putting your research project together, to make sure that you are familiar with the requirements for a successful project.

**2**

# HOW TO FIND AND USE EXISTING RESOURCES

Much background research has already been done for you. This section is designed to help you find the relevant material and use it effectively for your own project. This should provide you with research skills that will enable you to develop proper methods of researching existing data, whether it is historical, current news, statistics or other routinely generated information. This section should give you a better idea of how to go about your own work, and it should alert you to problems that might arise, thus making you an informed and efficient researcher. We will guide you to research already published, and provide you with expertise in how to prepare and present this data in your research project.

## (i) Using a library

The first task you must learn is how to use libraries, one of your most accessible resources, to their greatest advantage. Having done this you will then be able to access existing research and use it to *your* advantage. Libraries can be used for browsing, reading, researching, and borrowing. But some libraries can be intimidating places if you are not aware of how they operate, so let us look at the workings of libraries, the first port of call for anyone undertaking research at any level. Libraries can be small, medium, large and very large. They can be for specific purposes or for general use, for private, public or educational use, or all of these. They are all valuable places to find information. Many schools, companies, government departments and other organisations have their own specialised libraries.

*A library is one of the most accessible resources.*

### What is a library?

The *Penguin English Dictionary* says a library is 'a collection of books; [a] place where books are kept and can be consulted; [an] establishment containing books which can be borrowed by the public or members of an association; [a] series of books of similar kind issued by the same publisher.' So libraries are more than just places to borrow books for leisure reading. The *Encyclopaedia Britannica* has ten pages devoted to its description of a library, so it seems clear that a library is more than just a collection of books.

Indeed, libraries contain fiction and non-fiction books, reference books, journals, magazines, newspapers, audio-visual material, computer access, special collections and many useful services for readers. Larger libraries are designed to house all these facilities in different parts of the building. These libraries should have a prominently-displayed map of the different sections and their locations. See an example in Figure 2.1.

All libraries consist of different sections depending on their primary function.

## Different types of libraries

**A public community library** would cater for the needs of the general public by having a children's section as well as adult fiction and non-fiction books. It may also have a section with large-print books, and a collection of books and other material on audio cassette for people with sight problems as well as for general users.

**A municipal library** would also have a small reference section, a collection of magazines and newspapers, and reader services including catalogue enquiries and a photocopier.

**A larger academic library** needs to cater for students and researchers and consequently must have a larger reference section and a comprehensive collection of journals to keep up-to-date with the latest research. An audio-visual section would also be necessary to cater for the growing amount of material that comes only in microform. The general stock of books on all subject areas is classified according to the Dewey system. An extensive photocopying facility would be another essential requirement, as would a computer data search capability and an interlibrary loan facility.

**The National and State library** have a special purpose to fulfil as they are the holders of irreplaceable historic material which can generally be called the nation's heritage. Their duty is to preserve this material in the best possible condition for future generations. The material would consist of papers, diaries, maps, photographs, pamphlets, books and newspapers. Not all this material is available to be looked at because it may be fragile or secret for some reason. In general this type of collection is called the ARCHIVES, a place where historical records are kept and documents preserved. These libraries also have extensive book collections open to the general public, but they are not lending libraries. Most of the books are in closed stacks and you must ask staff to find them for you.

*Search out specialised libraries — they can be very useful to the researcher.*

Other specialised libraries would contain collections specific to a particular company or government department. For example, research departments would hold material relevant to their particular field of interest. Legal institutions would house law collections; companies, particularly large ones, would hold all the company records for a long period of time, perhaps since the company was established so that the history of the company could be preserved.

Figure 2.1    Deakin University library plan

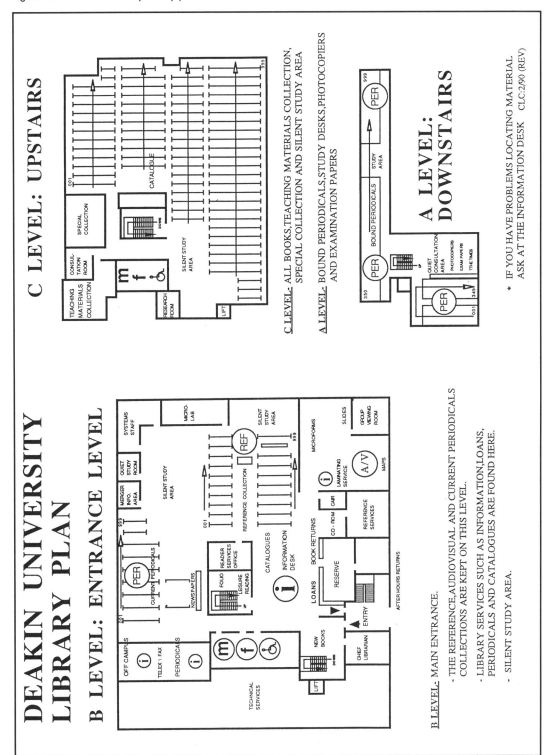

## Inside a library

Let's look at the inside of the library. Any library will have a main stack of fiction and non-fiction books. These are the parts of the library.

**The reference section:** This contains reference books such as encyclopaedias, yearbooks, dictionaries, atlases, bibliographies, indexes, abstracts, statistics, government publications and other research material. These books are not to be borrowed from the library but may be used in the library so that as many people as possible may have access to them.

**The periodical section:** A periodical is a magazine or journal that is published on a regular basis, e.g. weekly, monthly, annually. Periodical collections vary in size and content. University libraries have a large number of periodicals in many subjects, and there would probably be a separate list, usually computer-generated, to keep it up-to-date easily. The list would be revised each year and would be in alphabetical order by title. Periodical collections would cover a wide range of topics depending on the needs of any particular library. Overseas as well as Australian titles would be common, and topics from science to humanities would be necessary. 'Hansard' (parliamentary debates) from both federal and state parliaments, newspapers, magazines, scientific journals, historical studies and legal publications would be standard in most large libraries. The current year's issues are held in one area of the library and older issues are bound together and stored separately. Periodicals or journals usually contain major articles, book reviews and general information about specific subjects. Some journals are of general interest; (e.g. *Journal of Australian Studies*); some are highly specific (e.g. *Journal of Reproductive Technology*).

Most libraries would have a range of daily newspapers for patrons to read. However they probably only keep them for a few weeks or a few days because of space limitations. Larger libraries would have a microform collection of newspapers which allows a complete set to be held in one place. Local newspapers and historic newspapers may also be available. Some old newspapers have been produced in facsimile form or as a series in book form. This is sometimes a historical anniversary project, e.g. a centenary edition.

**Audio-visual section:** This section would include collections of microform material, video cassettes, audio cassettes and colour slides. A brief description of each of these collections follows.

Microform — This is a technique for storing large amounts of material by photographing it and reducing it in size. It is produced in two different forms — microfiche and microfilm. These allow a library to hold vast quantities of material in a much smaller area than the original material would take up, e.g. collections of newspapers that would take up vast storage space if collected in original form but on microfilm take up one filing cabinet or half a shelf. It also allows material which is in fragile condition to be accessed. Material which is viewed a lot need not deteriorate from overuse.

Microfiche takes the form of 150 x 105 mm transparencies containing up to 100 pages of information, depending on the size of the original page and the degree of reduction. The title and reference code is across the top of the microfiche. They are stored for protection in envelopes, arranged in number order in boxes on the library shelves. See Figure 2.2. To view the item you wish to look at, there are machines called readers that will magnify and project onto a screen the image recorded on the microfiche. See Figure 2.3. The material is viewed from left to right or from top to bottom but the microfiche can be searched quickly by scanning the edges of the fiche, then searching the appropriate column, rather than reading every page; this takes some practice. See Figure 2.2.

Microfilm is a film strip, again miniaturising the source for storage, access and preservation purposes. The film is threaded into a reading machine and viewed on a screen as with the microfiche. Microfilms are stored in boxes in series, and the catalogue call number of both microforms is prefixed with letters designating audio-visual material.

Figure 2.2   Audio-visual mircofiche

(a) Microfiche                    (b) Microfiche box storage

Video or audio cassette collection — This may be simply for borrowing, but in some larger libraries you may be able to view or listen on the premises, using TV monitors and tape recorders with headphones in desk areas, probably with the facility for multiple viewing or listening. The extent of the collection may depend on the library's size and scope.

Slide collections are housed in cases or drawers. A glass-covered light source is provided for viewing the slides. It may or may not be possible to borrow these items, depending on the particular library.

Figure 2.3   Microfiche and microfilm readers

Microfiche goes between glass under lens.

There are different magnifications.

(a) Microfiche reader

Microfilm feeds onto spool under lens.

There are different magnifications

(b) Microfilm reader

Photocopy facilities for both microforms are available with some machines.

**The reserve desk** contains books and articles that are necessary for current courses at tertiary institutions. As students need this material constantly, their use of this material is restricted in the library for a specified time, say one or two hours.

Interlibrary loans are available between many libraries, both academic and municipal. You fill out a form giving exact details of the book or article you wish to obtain. The request is then sent to another library that has this particular item, and either the item or a photocopy will be sent to the original library. This process takes several days or several weeks depending on where the book is located and whether it is in use, so keep this in mind when considering using this facility.

**Photocopy facility:** Most libraries have photocopiers. Machines may be operated by coins or card tokens, or in some cases operated by library staff. Most university libraries have a number of machines for student use as there is a heavy demand for photocopying books and other material as part of the students' regular course work. Some machines can reduce and enlarge; some have duplex facility, which allows both sides of the paper to be used. Automatic operation is available on some machines.

Microform machines may also have photocopying facility allowing you to obtain a printed copy of the microfiche or film version.

### How to find a book

Now we need to look at how a library stores its collection. To find a particular book or obtain a book on a particular subject, you need to have a system that tells you where you can locate it. CATALOGUING and CLASSIFI-CATION of the collection are the ways that have been devised to accomplish this. By these methods, it is possible to know what books are in a library and where to find them.

*If you are lost or in doubt, seek help from the library staff.*

Cataloguing involves recording the author, title and subject of all the books, and classification involves numbering and ordering the books systematically. The most common system of classification is called the Dewey system which uses ten broad areas numbered as follows:

100   Philosophy and related areas
200   Religion
300   The social sciences
400   Language
500   Pure sciences
600   Technology (applied sciences)
700   The arts
800   Literature and rhetoric
900   General geography and history

Within each of these sections there are sub-divisions which classify a book on any subject. For example, an Australian history book would be located at 994. This number is the CALL NUMBER of the book — it is the book's address or home on the library shelves.

**The library catalogue:** A catalogue is simply a list of items in a designated order. In this case it is a list of books in alphabetical order. A library catalogue can come in a number of forms including card, microfiche and computer. Irrespective of the format of the catalogue, certain fundamental information is included which enables any book to be located by author, title or subject. This is called cross referencing — where any book will be recorded at least three times — often more — under author, title and subject headings.

- Card catalogue. A catalogue entry on a card includes the call number, author, title, publisher, year published, subject, details about the book such as number of pages, whether there are illustrations, an index, or photographs etc. Each book has at least three separate card entries.
- Microfiche catalogue. A catalogue entry on microfiche includes all the same details that are found on the card system. The advantage of this system is that it is possible to scan many more entries at the one time. The catalogue also takes up far less space that a card catalogue.
- Computer catalogue. The computer catalogue again contains the same

information as the other systems, but also often provides information on the current status of the book, i.e. whether it is 'on loan', 'on shelf' or 'on hold'. You can search for an author's total output as a sequential entry, or search a subject by sub-headings using certain keywords. As well as this, the catalogue can be updated continually as the library acquires new publications.

There are other catalogue systems on computer that can access collections at other libraries.

Most libraries have information booklets and enquiry desks where staff can help you. Don't hesitate to ask them if you need help.

## (ii) How to use books and articles

This section aims to teach you methods of efficient and effective reading so that you are focusing on specific areas, not reading so widely that you have no time left for research. The secret is to find the parts of a book or article which are most relevant to your research — from general references to specific issues.

Depending on your topic or the progress of your research, you may need to read generally about a subject using an encyclopaedia, for example, or you may need to read very specifically about a particular idea using a specialised periodical on the subject.

### General reading

Having found your way into the library, overcome your intimidation, fought your way through the catalogue system, and now have a basic knowledge of where the various sections are to be found — heaven forbid you might even be able to locate a book on the shelves — congratulate yourself! You have made a major breakthrough!

*Allow time in your research programme for this time-consuming activity.*

Now you need to be able to use the books and articles that you can locate. Books which are available are reference books, general subject books, specific topic books. Reference books would include encyclopaedias, dictionaries, yearbooks, bibliographies, abstracts and indexes, atlases and other publications of resource material. Let us look at them in more detail.

**An encyclopaedia** is a book or a set of books of general information, usually arranged alphabetically by subject. Although the information is of a general nature, there are encyclopaedias varying from wide to narrow focus, for example, the *Encyclopaedia Britannica* contains world-wide information on a multitude of subjects, so it can provide general knowledge on a subject.

American or Australian encyclopaedias would contain general information either solely or largely about those countries; other encyclopaedias might be devoted to science or humanities or art.

**Dictionaries:** The most obvious are the English language dictionaries which come in many forms from a simple pocket version to huge multi-volume sets such as the twelve volumes of the *Oxford Dictionary*. However, it is usually not necessary to use a large dictionary when a simple one will do. The simplest dictionary will provide you with definition of word, a pronunciation guide, the functional classification (e.g. noun), and usually a word history. This information will be sufficient for all but the most complex of words.

There are, however, many other types of dictionaries that might be useful in research projects. For instance, we are all familiar with the standard English language dictionaries such as the *Macquarie, Oxford, Penguin*, etc. There are also English – other language dictionaries, thesauri catering for synonyms and other word usage, dictionaries of science, politics, Australian history, biography, literature, music, and many more. All such dictionaries are listed alphabetically and contain specialised information that is easy to find. A very useful source for Australian historical research is the *Australian Dictionary of Biography*. (See Annotated Bibliography.)

**Yearbooks** are annual publications containing information for one year. They may contain statistics, biographical notes, government or geographic features. Australia has yearbooks from all states, and a Commonwealth version which contains population statistics, economic, geographic, agricultural, commercial, financial, transport, and other information for either Australia or specific states. Most Commonwealth and state yearbooks have been published for more than fifty years, so they are a source of historical as well as current data.

**Bibliographies** are simply alphabetical lists of books or other publications on particular subjects. For example there is a bibliography of Australian literature, a bibliography of political science. They may be compiled by author or title or both. Some are ANNOTATED which means they have a brief description of the contents of the work. They can cover broad general subjects or specific subjects, and some are cumulative, which means that they are added to periodically, giving a continuous collection over a long period.

**Abstracts and indexes** are volumes that direct you to information in journals in particular years. They give bibliographical data, and abstracts also give a brief SYNOPSIS of the content of the article. There are both general and specific types and some are also cumulative to provide a comprehensive source of current, up-to-date knowledge for researchers. An example of a general index is the *Australian Public Affairs Information Service*, known commonly as APAIS. It has indexes to subjects and authors to access the articles, and covers broad subject areas of social science and humanities in Australia. It is published monthly. Specific indexes can be found for a multitude of subjects from Australian history to newspapers to medical research.

**Atlases and maps** are available in most libraries. Atlases come in many and varied forms. Some simply provide maps; others have text to accompany the maps. Still others might include DEMOGRAPHIC information about population, geological features, and other general data on a particular area. There are special types of atlases called social atlases that plot statistical material over geographic areas thus giving a graphic representation of housing, occupation, or income data from census figures. The *Social Atlas of Melbourne* is one of these. Several different series of topographical maps are available which are numbered according to a national grid. Check for these with your library, or go to a specialist map supplier for maps about your area of interest.

**Other references:** This is by no means an exhaustive list of reference books, but you can get some idea of the scope of information that is available to you. A useful book to obtain further information on reference books is Lane, Nancy D., *Techniques for Student Research: a practical guide*, Longman Cheshire, Melbourne, 1989.

You must not underestimate the use you can make of accessible books such as telephone books and street directories. The *Yellow Pages* contains lists of businesses, churches, schools, hotels etc. by location, giving the exact address. Street directories contain detailed maps of very specific areas, showing municipal boundaries, railway lines, tram routes, public amenities and recreation facilities. You can use these two sources of information for quite sophisticated research. For example, by plotting the location of hotels in a particular suburb it might be possible to see some correlation between transport facilities, historical development and the economic imperatives of an area.

Other useful sources of reference material have been produced as a consequence of our bicentennial year, 1988. In that year, there was a proliferation of publications about Australia and Australian society. A very useful and comprehensive reference collection is called *The Australians: a historical library*. It consists of eleven volumes covering the period from before 1788 to the present. It includes statistics, historical information, geographical and demographic material. It was written by a multitude of authors, all experts in their own field, and is a valuable resource for all students of Australia.

## Specific reading

General and specific topic books are the next port of call for researchers. You will be directed to them as you work through your research project, as you go from background reading to specific reading.

When you are exploring your research topic you will be confronted by academic books and periodical journals that you may not have encountered before. *Do not be daunted; they are not so difficult.* Look at Figures 2.4 and 2.5 for a description of these new publications. As you can see, they contain certain fundamental and similar parts, such as the main text, footnotes and a bibliography. The last two record the sources of information that have been used to produce the work. You should not read all of the main text of the book or the article until you are completely satisfied that it is of particular relevance to your topic.

---

**How to avoid over-reading**

There are three ways to reduce the amount of reading for a research project:
1. Narrow the focus of your project.
2. Read selectively for that subject.
3. Don't be sidetracked by other interesting information.

---

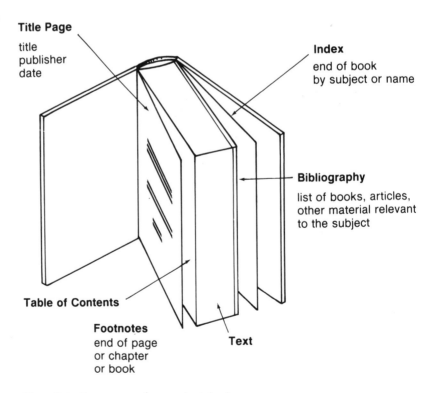

**Title Page**
title
publisher
date

**Index**
end of book
by subject or name

**Bibliography**
list of books, articles,
other material relevant
to the subject

**Table of Contents**

**Footnotes**
end of page
or chapter
or book

**Text**

Figure 2.4   The anatomy of an academic book

Figure 2.5    The anatomy of a periodical

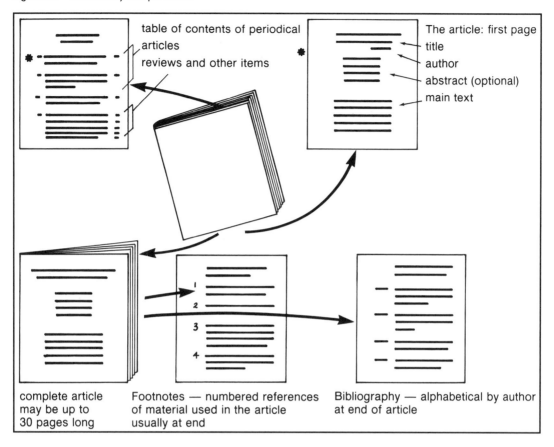

*Remember to read selectively.* Here is a useful exercise that will only take about 5 or 10 minutes but should save a lot of time in the long run.

1. Look at the contents page; take note of the sections, headings, etc.; get a feel for the emphasis the book takes.
2. Browse through the introduction.
3. Look at the index using keywords relevant to your subject or topic.
4. Look at the bibliography to see what other sources have been used.
5. Skim through the book looking at its presentation and graphic material.

This short exercise should give you a good idea if the book should be discarded or delved into more deeply. A similar approach can be taken when reading journal articles. There is sometimes, but not always, an abstract about the article which will give you a general idea of the content. The references (the footnotes and the bibliography) should give more clues for you to assess. Your best indication is the title of the article because in most journals it will be quite specific, and the journal in which it is located will indicate the area of study. Periodicals are also very good as a source of book reviews for that particular subject. In fact, part of most journals is set aside specifically for book reviews and they are indexed usually under the book title as well as under the name of the reviewer.

**Government publications:** Some are dull compilations of facts, a few are exciting, but almost all have lots of information. They relate to both the parliamentary section of government and the departmental (operational) section of government. Government means all levels — local, state and federal.

The parliamentary section would primarily be concerned with the daily recording of the proceedings of the state and federal Parliaments in both upper and lower Houses, known as Hansard. Hansards are printed daily when the House sits. They are a permanent record of the parliamentary proceedings, and are a vital resource as far as government is concerned. In theory, the people have access to the running of Parliament by this publication. The Hansard for the federal Parliament records all debates that were conducted in the House, and questions, answers, personal explanations, ministerial statements and passing of legislation. An index is available, recording the MP's name, subjects of debate, date and official number. All sections have a specific number which can be quoted.

**Annual reports of government departments** are also important sources of information which include details of the running of the department for that year, personnel, statistics, funding, research undertaken etc. Departments might publish other items relating to their specific section as occasional papers or research papers. For a list of guides to government publications consult the Annotated Bibliography. Other published reports would relate to specific committees or royal commissions, for example the Royal Commission into Aboriginal Deaths in Custody. (See D. H. Borchardt in the Annotated Bibliography for a guide to enquiries.)

The complete proceedings of all parliaments, state and federal, have been recorded and are available in bound form in most university libraries as well as major state libraries. These record all debates, votes and proceedings of both Houses. Generally they are indexed, although in some cases the indexes can be less than helpful. The state government *Gazettes* are available in bound form dating from the earliest times. They are the official proceedings of government and its function as a legislative body; as such they contain all official public service notices. Each state has a Public Record Office where state and local government documents are housed for preservation in archive collections.

*Some libraries house goverment publications in specific sections. Ask for help if you need it.*

**Electoral resources:** Electoral data are published regularly. These would include:
- electoral rolls which record the eligible voters for particular electoral areas;

- election results;
- analysis of results of particular elections;
- polls concerning leadership or other issues;
- referendum questions;
- constitutional matters.

Statistics are available relating to both state and federal election results. Very precise figures are available, such as the figures for particular polling booths for many years. There is wide scope for the use of these statistics: voting patterns for particular areas by state, region, town; informal voting patterns; separate party voting; particular candidate voting.

**Opinion polls:** Opinion polls are conducted on a regular basis by private companies on a wide variety of subjects. The ones we are probably most familiar with are the leadership polls which are printed in newspapers and magazines and interpreted by commentators. Most large libraries would carry copies of polls by companies such as Gallup, Roy Morgan or Saulwick. Some newspapers commission their own polls. A word of warning — when trying to analyse the results of opinion polls of any kind, you must study the questions very carefully; even the order in which the questions are asked may influence the result.

**Australian Bureau of Statistics:** The ABS, as it is known, is the government's own department for collecting and disseminating statistics about the population of Australia generally. Each state has an ABS office which is accessible to all the community, in person, by phone or by letter. It is possible to obtain statistical information on many aspects of Australian society.

The information is collected every five years in a census which the government undertakes. The information is generated in a variety of forms: pamphlets, books, computers, microform. Each year a catalogue is prepared listing all information that has been published. The scope of the ABS is almost unlimited. Here are some of the matters covered:

Population and housing

General and specific demographic statistics including births, deaths, marriages

Immigration, population trends and projections

Social statistics: education, health, welfare and social services

National account, finance and foreign trade

Labour statistics: workforce, earnings, conditions of employment, prices, consumer income/expectations

Agricultural statistics: livestock, crops and pastures

Agricultural finance

Fishing

Secondary industry and distribution

Manufacturing
Retail and wholesale trade
Tourism
Mining
Building and construction
Transport
General statistics
Transport services
Motor vehicle accidents.

*Be aware that if you approach ABS directly, costs may be incurred, however many libraries hold copies of ABS publications.*

The statistics are presented as computer print-out. These may be analysed in ways which can be useful to many research interests. They are usually recorded for geographical regions called LOCAL GOVERNMENT AREAS (LGA).

Historical statistics are available on microfiche and include birth, death and marriage statistics, yearbooks, government gazettes. These are classified by State — Vic., S.A., W.A., Tas., Qld., N.S.W.

**How to use statistics:** Statistics are numerical facts collected systematically. They may be simple tables of numbers, but a different form of presentation may show them more clearly or impressively, for example, bar or line graphs, spot graphs or pie charts. Examples of these are in Figure 2.6, or they can be plotted geographically using cross-hatching, colour-coding or shading on a map. Consider when numbers provide the most relevant comparative analysis: the MEAN number is the average; MEDIAN number is the number in the middle; and the MODE is the number that occurs most frequently. Decide which is more appropriate for each case.

There are more complicated analyses of statistics using arithmetical formulae but these are not relevant here. A book on statistical analysis would be the place to find more detailed information if it is required for your particular analysis. (See Annotated Bibliography)

# (iii) Newspapers and the electronic media

The most easily-accessible sources of information are newspapers, TV and radio. Every day you probably read a newspaper, watch some television and listen to the radio. If you follow some rules and are sensible about your interpretation of the information you can get, these forms of media can be useful resources for research. Here is a guide in how to use and analyse newspapers, TV and radio for social research projects.

They are primarily forms of communication and as such are a mirror of Australian society. You can gauge social attitudes and cultural values, among other things, by an appropriate analysis of these media. They may be used in a variety of ways to provide material for many different projects

Figure 2.6   How to use statistics in graphic form

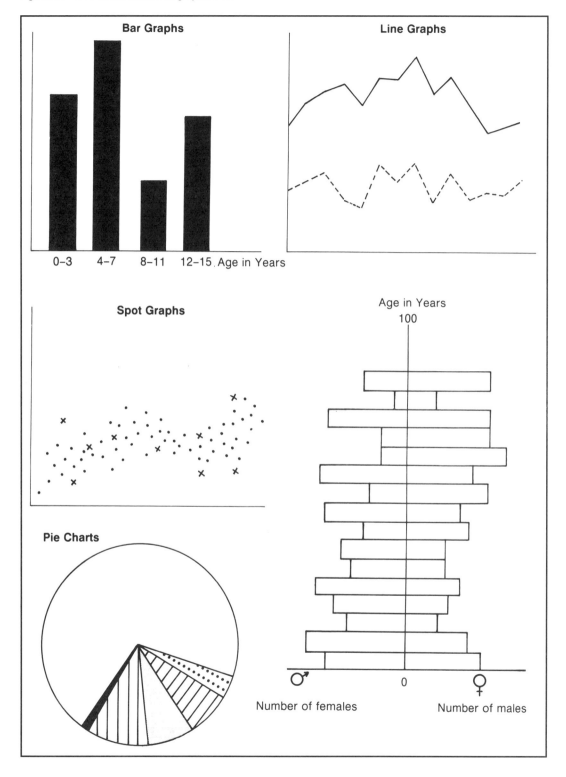

about Australian society. As an every-day resource they are sources of current news, cultural values, society opinion, but they may present a variety of interpretations which you should treat cautiously and carefully.

## Newspapers

There are many types of newspapers — local, regional, state, ethnic and national. You should be able to buy or order most newspapers from your local newsagent. (See Figure 2.7.) You would need to go to a large state or university library to find interstate and international newspapers. There may be an index to *The Times* (London) or *The Times Literary Supplement* in these large libraries. Old newspapers and previous issues of current newspapers are also available at university or state libraries on microfilm.

Special-interest groups may have their own newspapers; for example, trade unions, political parties, farmer organisations, Aboriginal groups and other community groups. Look in the Yellow Pages of a capital city telephone directory under 'Newspapers' and 'Magazines' to see the range available. Many groups also distribute newsletters which are brief and irregular publications and are sources of specific information for members of those organisations.

Figure 2.7   Types of newspapers

| **Examples of types of newspapers:** | |
| --- | --- |
| **Local:** | *Geelong News, Yarram Standard News, Wedderburn Express* |
| **Regional:** | *Hamilton Spectator, Latrobe Valley Express, The Examiner* (Launceston), *Illawarra Mercury* (Wollongong), *Centralian Advocate* (Alice Springs) |
| **State:** | *The Age* (Vic.), *Sydney Morning Herald, The West Australian, Hobart Mercury, The Queensland Times, The Advertiser* (S.A.) |
| **National:** | *The Australian, The Australian Financial Review* |
| **Weekly:** | *Business Review Weekly, The Weekly Times, Trading Post* |
| **Monthly:** | *The Independent Monthly* |
| **International:** | *The Times* (London), *Washington Post, Pacific Islands Monthly* |
| **Ethnic:** | *Jewish News, Il Globo, Australian Chinese Daily, Neos Kosmos* |

*Newspapers are an easily accessible source that can be over-used.*

**Using newspapers as a research tool.** Newspapers can be either primary or secondary sources, depending on the use to which you put them. If you use newspapers for background reading to gain information on a particular topic, they are SECONDARY SOURCES. If you use them as the main focus of your research, they are PRIMARY SOURCES. The most obvious material which may be obtained from newspapers is current news. News reporting, however, will be treated in different ways by different papers since there is a range from 'popular' to 'quality' newspapers. Because there is this variation, you must be cautious about your interpretation and be sceptical enough to question some of the opinions or bias that these articles may contain. We will discuss content analysis later in this chapter.

Newspapers contain many different sources of information:

*daily news:* an obvious source of information about the current news — local, national, international.

*advertising:* can give interesting information about current prices of goods, or in older newspapers, could give information about aspects of the material culture of the time.

*cartoons:* these can provide succinct social comment, and can be studied as examples of graphic style.

*computers:* there are feature articles, advertisements for hardware and software, and advertisements for jobs requiring computer skills.

*editorials:* often you can detect the editorial or political bias of a newspaper from a study of a range of its editorial articles.

*education:* there are articles for students about aspects of the curriculum of various subjects, pieces on study and examination skills, articles for teachers on developments in the field of education, and much more.

*employment advertisements:* these can be the source of useful statistical information, but you will have to do quite a bit of work to gather the information.

*feature articles:* it could be possible to focus on a particular area or community group through newspapers, for example, Aboriginal, rural communities, or ethnic communities. Feature articles usually delve into a subject in more detail than is done in general reporting.

*finance:* these pages contain far more detailed and accessible information than they did a few years ago, as well as graphs of economic indicators, stock market statistics and banking data.

*food:* recipes, maybe a 'Best Buy This Week' list, restaurant reviews and advertisements, and general articles about food all build up to a picture about the changing role of food in the daily life of people.

*gardening:* there is usually a weekly gardening column in most larger newspapers. This can be a useful source of information on changing trends, for example the popularity of restoring old gardens, and environmental issues such as conservation.

*historical reprints:* these appear, sometimes on a regular basis, such as 'Famous Headline', or 'On This Day Fifty Years Ago'. A collection of these could be the basis of a useful historical collection. A historical milestone, such as a centenary, is usually a rich source of recollections, photographs, and old newspaper reprints.

*letters to the editor:* these are valuable sources of information on community attitudes.

*life-style:* in recent years these columns have been identified as such, but articles on similar topics have been published under other names in the

Figure 2.8  What's in a newspaper?

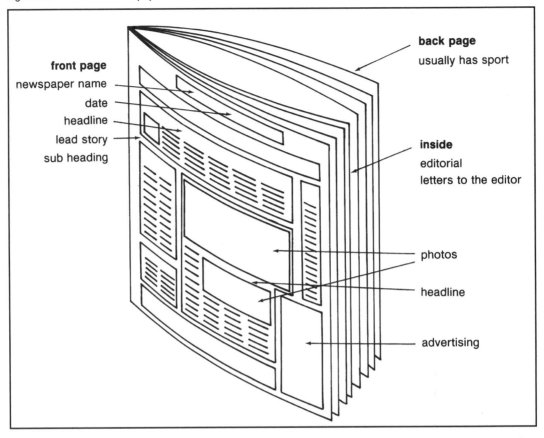

past. They are obvious sources of information about people's lives at that time.

*photojournalism:* consider the regular photos used to illustrate articles, as well as larger collections of photos on particular topics.

*real estate:* you could, for example, obtain property values for an area over a given period, or comparative values at, say, five-yearly intervals from a search of the real estate columns. Photographs or drawings of buildings can provide examples of the architectural styles of different eras.

*regular specific-topic columns:* weather reports, currency exchange figures, shipping arrivals and departures, times of church services and many other miscellaneous columns reveal the varying interests and needs of people.

*reviews of books, films, art:* most newspapers have these regular items in a particular section of the paper. They are usually written by the same people in each issue, so there is some continuity from one week to the next. Information can be gleaned, therefore, about the subject (the book, etc.), about the author and probably about a wider cultural framework.

*reviews of the past week's news:* provided as a summary for busy readers; you can use it as a form of an index to recent events.

*science:* regular articles appear on matters of scientific interest. It may be interesting to compare recent and older articles. Current issues — such as IVF technology, environmental concerns such as greenhouse and global warming — may be dealt with in detail.

*sport:* Always a great deal of information in almost every day's paper. Huge amounts of information about Olympic Games and major international, national and state competitions. Results, photos, predictions, programmes, articles on sportsmen and women, items on new equipment, etc. Comparisons could be made about the roles of women and men in sport, including their roles as participants, journalists and commentators.

*supplements:* from time to time, special sections appear about particular issues — small business, the transport industry, etc. Much information can be gained from these sources, and advertisements for related businesses can lead you to further local sources of information.

*women's pages:* these focus on issues of particular interest to women, for example, child care, equal pay, sexual discrimination.

**Compiling a newspaper collection.** This will depend on your type of research and the use you are putting your clippings to.

---

**Project**

You may need to collect:
• for a particular issue, e.g. Aboriginal land rights, multiculturalism, conservation, or
• for an event, e.g. a bicentennial or an election, or
• a pictorial collection of photos, cartoons.

Whatever your research, when you cut out your article, make sure to write on the article itself the name of the paper, the date and the page number, because you will need to acknowledge the source of your information in your project.

Finding the best method of storing your newsclipping collection depends on a number of factors:
• How many are you likely to collect?
• What is the scope or variety of the collection?
• What are you going to do with them?
• How long do you wish to keep them?

Collections of newsclippings, rather than being an *ad hoc* individual student activity, could be made into a major group research project with the result becoming an ongoing library resource for the school.

---

**Methods of storing and indexing.** Always record *sources* on each article — name of paper, date, page.

*Plastic envelopes:* One of the simplest ways of storage is to use plastic envelopes in a folder and label each envelope for a different subject.

Figure 2.9  Storing and indexing news clippings

*Scrap books:* Glue clippings in scrap books in chronological order using different books or sections of books for separate subjects. A tag attached at the side of the pages for clear visibility is an easy way of indexing them.

*Large collections:* Glue each clipping on a separate page with newspaper, date, page and index subject on top of each page. Store them in binders in chronological order; list index in alphabetical order. Newsprint and glue both deteriorate with time, so consider photocopying the material if you intend to keep the collection for more than a year or so. Indexing large collections may be done by general headings, e.g. Aborigines, Art, Gold, Work, or by headings with sub-headings, e.g. Aborigines — Culture. See Figure 2.9.

**Content analysis.** An analysis of the content of newspapers can be carried out in a number of ways depending on the needs of your research project. Whether you are studying newspapers themselves and their function as communicators of news to the community, or newspaper articles for their particular content and interpretation, a content analysis can be devised to cater for your needs. General or specific analyses are both legitimate ways to go about your research. The following are different ways to approach the problem:

*A 'general analysis' of coverage by calculating the amount of space taken up by a particular news item*

The measure of the importance of a news story can be calculated by recording the amount of space a particular story is given. An important issue such as the war in the Persian Gulf or the financial collapse of the Pyramid Building Society produces many different forms of coverage such as articles, editorials, features, graphics, and letters to the editor. To analyse these in a general way in order to make comparisons between papers, measure the length of the columns taken up by the different stories by using a ruler. See Figure 2.10.

Also take into account the page number that the articles are printed on; this is also significant as a measure of the relative importance of the story. The number of cartoons and photographs accompanying the story are also worth recording for comparative analysis.

*Specific analysis of particular articles for their interpretation of issues of contemporary importance*

This can be a useful way to analyse an article for its content and examine how it can be related to the wider context of Australian society, for example, gender, ethnicity and class. Select articles appropriate to your project's theme.

Several readings of the articles may be necessary. A preliminary reading should be followed by a more detailed analysis of the article, paragraph by paragraph. Write a few sentences making a general statement of the issue as it relates to contemporary Australian society; for example, the debate about the ordination of women is about issues of gender and power in a religious framework.

Having decided on the main issue, identify the focus of the arguments given in the article. It should be possible to decide whether the article gives a biased view by taking a particular side in the argument, or if a balanced approach is presented, giving points for and against. Most difficult issues are complex, having many important and equally valid points of view to take into account.

With most articles the writing should progress with consistency and continuity and therefore the arguments should be able to be followed logically. Analyse each paragraph, making a brief summary as you go.

*Analysis of the relationship of headlines to news items*

An analysis of headlines should include:

- size of type as a measure of the importance of the news item
- the relationship of the headline to the article, and the use of sub-headings
- a comparative analysis of similar articles in different newspapers.

Figure 2.10   Analysis of a newspaper front page

size of headlines can be measured

Amount of space allocated to a news item can be measured in column cms.

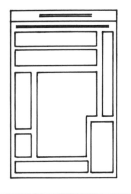

Front page divided for analysis
and measurement

Take a major issue and compare the headlines for it in more than one newspaper. Consider in your analysis whether the headline is a correct indication of the content of the article, or is there another purpose for it, such as to attract attention. If the issue goes on for several days or weeks, does the emphasis change over time? Do the newspapers treat issues differently? Look at the treatment of political, entertainment and regional matters. See Figure 2.10.

*Comparative analysis of issues by different newspapers*
This will require you to do specific analyses of articles from different papers about similar issues. You could choose national, major city daily, and regional papers to get a sampling of papers with different background emphasis. The analysis of specific articles has been dealt with in an earlier section, so follow the same procedure. Make a brief synopsis of the main points of the articles, and analyse the emphasis of the article. You may find that articles on particular issues have a regional bias.

*Readership analysis*
It is possible to obtain statistics on the people who read particular newspapers. You can also do a survey for yourself. (See section on surveys, pp 58-68.)
   Try to analyse people by:
 • age,
 • gender,
 • work/employment,
 • home suburb or town,
 • ethnic background.
   When you analyse the results, it may be possible to make a judgement about the target audience of newspapers.

*Relationship of paper ownership and editorial content*
This will require you to read the editorials of several different newspapers for a prolonged period of time, looking at a variety of issues. The specific analysis of articles is dealt with earlier in this section (Content analysis).
   Ownership of newspapers can be a complicated business; some are owned by independent people or companies, while others are tied to networks. Analysis of bias may be easy to interpret or it may be rather more obscure. Recently ownership of newspapers has become a major political issue. Dynamic changes have occurred and will probably continue. For a good summary of the 1991 state of media ownership see *The Age* special feature called 'The Media: a special report on ownership and control' (Monday 5 August 1991). This supplement contains detailed analysis of the main issues including political framework, foreign ownership, media bias as well as basic statistical material. Bear in mind that some of the informa-

Figure 2.11  Tabulation of content analysis

|  | Age | Herald-Sun | The Australian |  |  |  |
|---|---|---|---|---|---|---|
| Real estate |  |  |  |  |  |  |
| Economics |  |  |  |  |  |  |
| Art |  |  |  |  |  |  |
| News |  |  |  |  |  |  |
| Sport |  |  |  |  |  |  |
| Classifieds |  |  |  |  |  |  |

tion may be already out of date, but it is a good overall look at the issue and an excellent starting point.

*Space allocation of categories*
This analysis can be done by measuring the column-centimetres of articles in sections such as sport, news, real estate, economics, classified advertisements. Analysis and recording could be tabulated. See Figure 2.11.

*Use of graphics in newspapers*
Graphics can mean photographs, cartoons and other illustrations used to enhance the newspaper articles. Analysis of photographs can be made by a critical examination of the photo used to illustrate a news item. An analysis of the use of photos of prominent public figures could be made, such as well-known politicians. Do editors use any old photo or graphic, or do they choose very carefully to illustrate a news story in a particular way? Cartoons could be analysed in a comparative way by collecting a series from each of several different papers. Consider how they are used. Do they focus on:
- humour,
- sex or gender,
- politics,
- caricature, or
- sarcasm.

Note where the cartoons are used (the front page, or elsewhere), and consider the impact this has on the readers. (See Figure 2.12.)

## The electronic media — Television
Television is often criticised for its content, presentation, and the detrimen-

Figure 2.12   Use of graphics

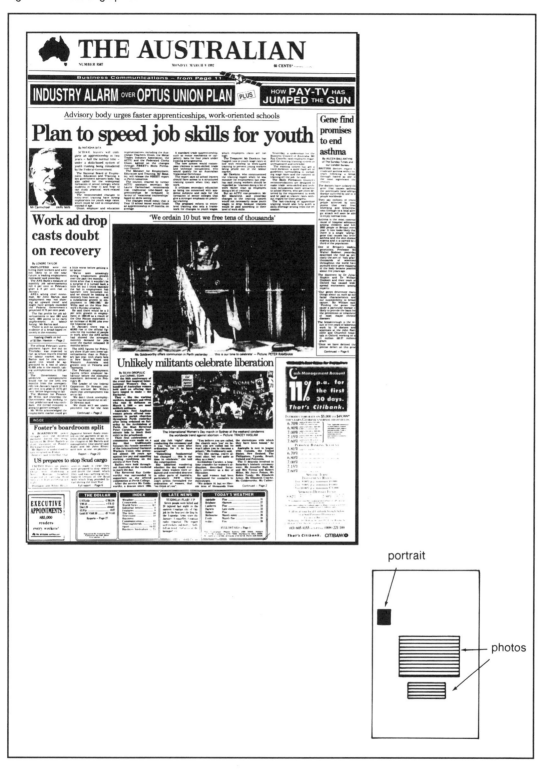

portrait

photos

*Further reading:
Donald E. Stewart,
The Television
Family: a content
analysis of the
portrayal of family
life in prime time
television,
Australian Institute
of Family Studies,
Melbourne, 1983.*

tal impact it has on society. Here is an opportunity to give it a better image and appreciation. After all, the most accessible form of information-gathering is right in your living-room — your television set. *But* you must be a discerning and perceptive viewer, not merely a sponge, soaking up everything. *You must be selective.*

What television has to offer is a multitude of programmes, from education to entertainment, which, if viewed with purpose and intelligence, can provide you as a researcher with much useful, indeed valuable, information about Australian society. We have, in Australia, both public and private channels available, giving (to at least the densely-populated areas of the country) a range of programming that is both wide in scope and varied in content. News, sport, film, drama, even advertisements, may be sources of information for studying Australian society.

**How to make the best use of television.** The most obvious sources of information are news bulletins and current affairs programmes which, theoretically at least, should provide news and an analysis of the news. In many cases, the two programmes are linked together by being on adjacent time slots, or by having personnel in common; here are some examples:
- *ABC News*, followed by *The 7.30 Report*;
- *Channel 7 News*, followed by *Real Life*;
- *Channel 9 News*, followed by *A Current Affair*;
- *Channel 10 News*, followed by *Hinch*.

Some current affairs programmes, however, do have their own identity, e.g. *Four Corners, Couchman, 60 Minutes, Lateline.*

**News.** News can be dealt with in a variety of ways, and there are biases in television news-presenting that need to be remembered. News is a selective business, however, watching it is the best way of knowing of the day-to-day events of the state, the country and the world, and it must not be underestimated as a source of news.

When viewing news bulletins, you need to take account of both the *content* and the *presentation* of that news to appreciate the end product. The *content*, i.e. the actual news items presented, may vary for different channels. For example, a capital city station may place stronger emphasis on local matters relating to that particular capital city, while state and world news take a secondary place. Another station such as SBS, catering to the multicultural population of Australia, may give priority to world news, with Australian and local state issues in a secondary place.

The *presentation* of the news can vary from entertainment, drama, to purely factual. Indeed, a project could focus on the presentation of news; you could look critically at how the prospective audience influences the content and delivery of that service. Does the ratings system influence the content of news, or vice versa?

News on television is very often governed by the visual material available, although there would be some items of such importance that they would override this consideration, for example, a major military conflict would have to be covered even if no film or video was available; file images would be used. But if there were two stories of equal strength, one with and one without visual images, the one with visual material would go to air rather than the one without.

Compare print news, TV news and radio news, of the same issue and try to draw some conclusions from your comparison.

**Current affairs.** As with news programmes, there is a variety of current affairs programmes. These programmes analyse the news, look more closely at current issues, and explore different views on particular topics of interest. If you view several different current affairs programmes, you will find each will have its own distinctive format, and will probably be heavily influenced by either the on-camera personality or the editorial team. They will establish the guidelines which the programme adheres to in its presentation, content, and its overall style. The governing factor is probably the audience which the programme targets. If popularity ratings are the criteria upon which the programme is based, then the stories which go to air will reflect this. If the programme aims to attract the greatest number of viewers, this means catering to the 'lowest common denominator' by the use of sensationalism and entertainment.

Other programmes may focus on local issues and may deal with only two or three features per programme to treat each of them in more detail. Techniques used could include the provision of background information, interviews, debates, graphics, and even audience participation, where questions are put to guest speakers and an invited audience.

Some programmes may spend the whole programme focused on one topic which is of particular interest to the community, for example, the IVF debate, immigration, environmental issues, violence in society. Current affairs programmes on ethnic stations would reflect their audience.

• Compare and contrast news bulletins for a given period. View three or four different stations on one particular night. How is news treated by different stations?

• Compare and contrast current affairs programmes from different stations. What audiences do you think the programmes are directed to? Does ethnicity play a part in current affairs or news on all TV stations?

**Film and drama.** Australian movies and feature films can be used as a rich research resource. You would need to regularly search TV programme guides for relevant material, and you can also use video and library lending facilities for some titles. Contact the State Film Centre or your local library and ask if they have a list of suitable films.

Before viewing the movie, try to obtain as much information about it as you can. Look for film reviews, or see if it was based on a novel. This way, you can view it with advanced knowledge, and question the presentation as you go along. Some issues you may want to examine from this viewpoint are:

- How is Australian society portrayed in feature films?
- Is the Australian culture realistically portrayed?

**Sport.** Australian society and its relationship with sport are revealed on television. Sport is one of the main forms of recreation of Australians, and this seems to be reflected in the amount and range that is televised. There are several ways that a researcher could analyse this relationship through television coverage. Some questions to consider are:

- How is sport conveyed as an Australian institution on TV?
- Determine the percentage of hours devoted to sporting programmes, dividing the total up into:
  — replays;
  — discussion panels;
  — other.
- What percentage of the news is taken up by sport?
- What percentage of sport reporting is about (a) women, and (b) men?
- List all activities regarded as sport: e.g. car racing, football, cricket, golf, tennis, horse racing, etc. Which type of sport has the most coverage? Why?
- How does advertising influence or manifest itself in sport? What effect does sponsorship have on sport? Who are the main advertisers or sponsors?

**Advertising.** Much is said about the impact of advertising in Australian society. Television needs advertising to exist in its present form, as selling advertising time brings in revenue to buy or produce other programming, therefore it is necessary. As much as we might dislike or disapprove of advertising, it will always be a part of privately-funded television stations, so it should be used in a positive way. To research Australian society through advertising, you would need to survey the material, looking at the content, presentation, and the scope.

**Content analysis.** Content analysis of TV programming, as with newspapers, can be done in a systematic way by viewing, recording and analysing the results. A general analysis of programming of TV stations can be made by recording the programmes on particular nights for a designated period. This can be done by looking at a TV guide and recording the results in a table. (See Figure 2.11.)

Direct viewing can be undertaken as a group project, so that different people view different channels on the same evening. This allows for more data to be collected. The scope of your analysis could be very general or very specific. For example, you could make a broad analysis of the types of TV programmes or you could analyse a single type of show such as news and current affairs, or a specific programme like *The Flying Doctors* or *A Country Practice*.

Depending on your choice you will need to design a recording system for your particular needs, perhaps a form to be filled in on a regular basis. Maybe segments of programmes need to be timed, or advertising needs to be monitored. You may wish to record a programme for later analysis.

The content of advertisements can be analysed in a similar way by looking at them systematically. The amount of advertising on a particular channel over one evening might be a good project. Record the type of product each advertisement is promoting, the time of screening, the duration of the advertisements, the number of screenings, what programme each advertisement interrupts. Design a table to record this information, then make an appropriate analysis of the results. For example, you may consider the influence the advertisers have on particular groups such as children.

---

**Project**

Undertake a small-scale analysis of a particular programme over a set period. For example, study *A Country Practice* for an analysis of family and social values.

Determine a set number of episodes to view — maybe four or six, depending on the number of people helping you. Record details of characters, using age, gender, type of employment and ethnicity. Observe the show, and record the activities and attitudes of the characters relative to the overall plot.

The storyline can be analysed for the following topics:
- family,
- sex/romance,
- employment,
- current issues,
- morality,
- social/community opinion.

If these topics don't suit the programme you have selected, draw up a list which does.

---

## The electronic media — Radio

To a lesser extent radio programmes can be used to gather information about Australian society. The best way to start is to read a good radio guide to find if there are programmes relevant to your research. Radio programmes range from local community to regional and capital city stations. Radio Australia caters for international listeners, and most modern radios will allow you to listen to all these different types of broadcasts.

Besides music, radio programmes include news, current affairs, sport, and other specialised topics such as talkback, programmes on ethnic communities, Aboriginal/Koori interests, women's issues, political and legal matters, interviews, economics, science, religion, history, book reviews, and others.

As with TV, advertising is a significant part of radio broadcasting, and could be used to look into Australian society.

Parliamentary broadcasts have a special AM frequency which only operates when parliament is in session.

Using radio as a research tool may be more difficult to manipulate, but with a content analysis similar to that used with television by the recording and study of programming, it could be a useful medium. Simply adapt the charts in the TV analysis to suit your own research needs and try to think creatively about how society could be studied through the spoken word; for example, talkback programmes, while not truly representative of popular opinion, are, nevertheless, some gauge of attitudes from Australian society.

A useful place to start would be to make a comprehensive search of the radio section of newspaper media guides. Make sure you study a whole week of programmes to ensure that you notice all relevant types of programmes. From this you should be able to make an assessment of the value that this material will have for your particular research.

# (iv) Community

Your own community is a logical place to find out about Australian society. But there are some *do's* and *don'ts* that should be followed if you are to gain as much from the contact as you can.

Consult your teacher about how best to contact the community in your area. He or she may have organised some appropriate people for your course. There may be a resource list of people — employers, union people, etc., who are willing to be approached.

## Community resources
• People
• Local councils and political representatives
• Government departments
• Hospitals and charitable organisations
• Businesses and industry
• Art galleries, museums and libraries
• Special interest groups
• Universities
• Churches
• TV and radio stations

and the list can go on and on. For a comprehensive look at your particular community, use the local phone book's index. Government departments are in the front of the book and the *Yellow Pages*, which contains businesses, are at the back. (The Yellow Pages may be a separate publication depending on the size of the community.) Some local government bodies (councils) produce a community resource booklet.

**People.** Includes your family (immediate and extended), your school community (teachers, students, parents, members of the school council). Neighbours and the rest of your acquaintances should also be included, as well as the wider community.

**Local councils and political representatives.** If you have a political or parliamentary query, your local member of parliament, either federal or state may be able to help. Your local council probably has a citizen's advice bureau which would be able to direct you to sources of information which are accessible to you.

**Government departments.** Local, state and federal departments are entirely different organisations, so do not assume they deal with the same matters. Although there may be some overlapping of information, the jurisdiction of a state department relates to a particular state, whereas federal departments deal with Australia-wide matters. The importance of local government varies according to the size of the municipality and its particular needs. Check your phone book for departments.

**Hospitals and charitable organisations.** Ask your teacher. You may be able to obtain relevant information about these organisations by looking at their annual reports.

**Businesses and industry.** Some businesses may be willing for you to make direct contact but it may be more appropriate for your teacher to make contact for you. It may be better for you to contact the Victorian Employers' Federation (VEF) and the Australian Council of Trade Unions (ACTU) for general information on matters relating to work and workers.

**Art galleries, museums and libraries.** All of these places are convenient sources of information, as they are geared to public access.

**Special interest groups.** These groups include sporting, religious, ethnic, history and many more. A community guide book would list many in your particular community. If you require specific historical information about your locality, the local historical society would be a logical place to approach. Remember however that such groups are usually run by volunteers and have little money to deal with requests. Be prepared to offer them some help for the results of your research as a way of thanks.

**Universities.** As well as providing access to their libraries, universities also have centres which deal with specific types of research and data collections. The range and scope of the centres would depend on the particular expertise of the academic community of a particular faculty. Ring the secretary of the appropriate faculty and ask if a relevant centre is set up.

**Churches.** Your local community could consist of a wide range of Christian and non-Christian denominations, e.g. Anglican, Roman Catholic, Jewish, Russian Orthodox, Hindu etc. Some churches also have support groups attached to them and these may also prove to be sources of information.

**TV and radio stations.** Community groups can reach the public more widely via TV and radio. Community radio has a popular following in many places, so it is valuable source of information. Many TV stations have a community announcements segment which performs a valuable role.

### How can I contact them?

Letter ... telephone ... personal contact. The method of contact may depend on who you want to talk to and why. If it is someone you already

know, it might be appropriate to simply ask them face to face. For example, interviewing grandma probably doesn't need an appointment, but contacting other people may need a more formal approach. Making contact with your community would seem to be a simple matter. In theory this is true, but if you are trying to contact an organisation or someone who has responsibility in the community, it is a good idea to make a formal request as a matter of courtesy. A letter would be preferable in the first instance, to arrange for an appointment for a meeting, depending on your requirements. First locate their address and phone number from your phone book. You may need to make some phone calls first to find the most appropriate person to contact at a particular organisation. A letter directed to an individual may obtain quicker results than one simply addressed to a whole department, or organisation.

When writing to a government department, try to be sure that you are writing to the correct department. There are several ways of finding out:

- look it up in the phone book;
- enquire by phone first;
- ask the local MP's office.

Government administration is a complicated business and frequently subject to change, so make sure your information is as up-to-date as possible.

If your need to tap into the community is a complex one, a formal

Figure 2.13  Letter-writing

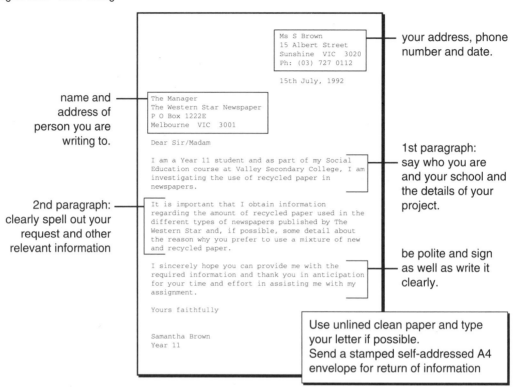

name and address of person you are writing to.

2nd paragraph: clearly spell out your request and other relevant information

```
                                    Ms S Brown
                                    15 Albert Street
                                    Sunshine  VIC  3020
                                    Ph: (03) 727 0112

                                    15th July, 1992

The Manager
The Western Star Newspaper
P O Box 1222E
Melbourne  VIC  3001

Dear Sir/Madam

I am a Year 11 student and as part of my Social
Education course at Valley Secondary College, I am
investigating the use of recycled paper in
newspapers.

It is important that I obtain information
regarding the amount of recycled paper used in the
different types of newspapers published by The
Western Star and, if possible, some detail about
the reason why you prefer to use a mixture of new
and recycled paper.

I sincerely hope you can provide me with the
required information and thank you in anticipation
for your time and effort in assisting me with my
assignment.

Yours faithfully


Samantha Brown
Year 11
```

your address, phone number and date.

1st paragraph: say who you are and your school and the details of your project.

be polite and sign as well as write it clearly.

Use unlined clean paper and type your letter if possible.
Send a stamped self-addressed A4 envelope for return of information

approach from the school or teacher may be required. For example, if you are examining a particular workplace, or perhaps comparing workplaces of different industries or companies, it would not be a good idea to arrive at the door of the building and ask to be shown around. Another approach might be to go to an organisation such as the Victorian Employers' Federation, the Australian Council of Trade Unions or Trades Hall to obtain information. They may be better geared up to deal with such requests, as public relations would be one of their roles.

**Letter-writing.** A letter should be clearly written, typed if possible, on white, unlined paper. It should have some fundamental information in it as well as your specific request. See Figure 2.13 for an example. You should send a self-addressed envelope of appropriate size as well, for your reply.

Remember that your letter may be one of many that this person or department receives, and that your request involves this person or department in additional work, so
• be courteous,
• be precise,
• be appreciative.
Also, remember that other students will come after you so please make

it as easy as possible for your request to be fulfilled. This may mean that the students after you may be treated favourably. If you make unreasonable requests, the next student may be knocked back. Always remember that your request *will* be one of many, so allow enough time for it to get through the proper channels. Do not expect a reply within the week; allow at least two weeks, or even longer for busy people.

**Telephone calls.** Use a current telephone directory to ensure you have the correct number. You may want to write a list of the points you need to make in your phone call, so you don't forget something important. When requesting information or appointments by phone, be sure you understand specifically what you want to know. If you are trying to make an appointment, be as flexible about time as you can. Try to give the person some idea of how long your interview needs to be. Be polite, be accurate, be precise. Remember to tell the answerer who you are, what you want and the reason for your request. If you are refused, don't be offended; you simply may have to think more about your research methods.

You may need to check a part of an interview — phone is usually the quickest way. Remember to have any relevant material close by to refer to, and always write up the details of your conversation immediately; do not rely on your memory; it is not always reliable. Record anything you think is relevant — time, date, name, details. *Always thank the person for their help.*

**Personal contact.** This will depend on how well you know the person you are about to see and the reason for your contact. If you know them well, for instance, members of the family or close friends, an informal conversation is probably appropriate. People you know slightly or not at all should be treated rather more formally. You will need to inform them of who you are and the purpose of your visit if you haven't already done so by letter; even refreshing their memory is probably a good idea anyway.

Work on the principle that if you are polite, forthcoming and honest with them, they will treat you the same way. Interview techniques are dealt with in Chapter 3. You will probably have only one chance for a meeting, so make sure if you have made an appointment with someone that you are on time and that you ask everything you wish to ask, because you might not get another opportunity. Be prepared before you go about what you want to ask this person. Make a list of your questions, and refer to it at the appointment. Make sure you have answers to as many of your questions as possible, but be brief. Your interviewee will have other things to do as soon as you go. At the end of your interview, thank the person for spending their time helping you.

Figure 3.3   Computer hardware and software

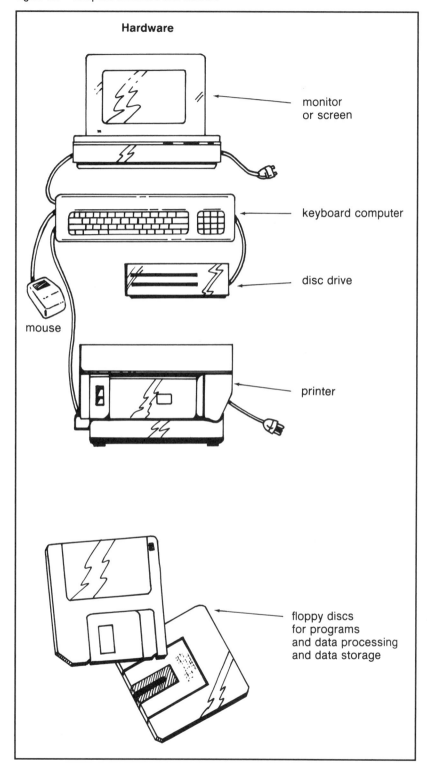

**Hardware**

monitor
or screen

keyboard computer

disc drive

mouse

printer

floppy discs
for programs
and data processing
and data storage

work it can handle, so take care to consider the usefulness of any particular package for you and your work.

You must have had enough practical experience in the use of the computer. It is not possible to instantly expect to be able to use them without having considerable practice or access to expertise to make operation easy and quick.

You must have access to the appropriate software and hardware. You may be fortunate enough to have a computer room at school, or better still, you may have access to one at home. Having compatible software is also a critical requirement.

If you think you would like to use computers for research, it would be worthwhile to set aside some time on a weekly basis to learn these skills. It will be of great benefit to you later on as well. Get some advice from your computer science teacher, and ask for books on the subject at your library.

*Word processing* software allows you to use your computer as a typewriter. It enables you to make corrections and alterations easily. However you can do many more things to process words, e.g.:

- type text;
- use different typefaces or sizes;
- move text around;
- create headings;
- design page layout;
- insert page numbers;
- insert footnotes;
- sort the bibliography alphabetically;
- print text.

*Graphics.* Software exists which allows you to use standard graphic design or to design your own.

*Database* software enables the compilation of data into a collection of information that can be indexed, arranged and retrieved in many useful ways. You can obtain packages which already contain relevant programs, but it is also possible to design programs to suit your particular needs. For example, there are family history programs designed to record individuals' specific details.

*Data analysis* software can be obtained which analyses statistical information by standard statistical methods; e.g. averages, means, random numbers, squared.

*Information networks.* These are networks that can be accessed to give information on a variety of subjects. One particular example would be a library information network. COOLCAT lists books and periodicals located at Victorian universities. CD-ROM (Compact Disk – Read Only Memory) is a fairly new way to store large amounts of information so that you can search a wide range of material quickly and easily. The information is stored on a compact disk, and it is accessed by a computer terminal and a printer. Large libraries would have several indexes in this format covering subjects such as medicine, history, sociology and education. There are Australian indexes on CD-ROM, including CDATA, which is a computer package allowing manipulation of Australian Bureau of Statistics material. Some guidelines will be needed to use the network successfully; this is available from the staff of your library.

This section is not a comprehensive guide to computer use in research. It does, however, give you some idea of the scope of computer technology so you can follow up the areas of interest for your particular need. *Don't be put off by technology.*

# (iii) Interviews and oral history

Interviewing involves asking questions of other people in order to gain knowledge. Interviews can be conducted on a one-to-one basis, or in a group situation where a small number of people contribute to the discussion. They can take many forms from informal chats between friends to formal meetings using structured questions.

| Steps in interviews and oral history |
| --- |
| 1.   Background research |
| 2.   Plan your questions |
| 3.   Decide who you are going to interview |
| 4.   Decide how you are going to record the interview |
| 5.   Contact the person(s) to be interviewed |
| 6.   Carry out the interviews |
| 7.   Transcribe and summarise your tapes |
| 8.   Analyse your results |

Recording your interview can also be done in a number of ways. Methods of analysis and interpretation are also many and varied. The decision about what type of interview is most appropriate is governed by a number of factors:

- **Why** should you interview?
- **Who** should you interview?
- **What** should you ask and how should you ask it?
- **How** should you analyse the interview?

## Why should you interview?

Think of the most newsworthy event that happened in your area lately. How did you first find out about it? Imagine that you have been asked to write an article about it for your school newspaper; make a list of the extra sources you would need to consult. How complete a picture would you have if you restricted yourself to using only written sources?

This simple exercise should serve to demonstrate some of the limitations of relying totally on written sources for information. Because of our reliance on telecommunication, and a certain guardedness about what is committed to paper, written records provide only a partial picture of the society in which we live. We need to be similarly guarded about records which have come down to us from the past. By their very nature, official records tend to tell us more about the victors than they do about the vanquished. Any history based solely on written sources will then tell us more about the rich than it does about the poor, more about the powerful than about the powerless. It will favour men over women, adults over children, and whites over blacks in the story which it tells of the past.

Oral history offers us the opportunity to redress some of this imbalance, just as asking questions will help you in finding out about any event or situation today. Often the people around you — your family, your neighbours and your friends — will be rich sources of information. However it is up to you to ask the right questions. That is why you need to master the art of interviewing.

## Who do you interview?

Having accepted that interviewing can both widen and democratise our sources of information, can you now set forth bravely, tape recorder in hand? Well, not quite. Before you set out you need to make some decisions about who you are going to interview and how you are going to judge the information which they provide.

With written sources you can use the library catalogue and then indexes and tables of contents to guide you in your search. With people it's a little more difficult, but the underlying question is the same. You are looking for someone who is in a position to know some of the answers to your research questions. You want first-hand evidence, not hearsay. If, for example, you wanted to find out what life was like in your town during the Second World War, there would be little point in interviewing your grandfather who signed up in 1939 and did not come home again until the war was over. Your grandmother would have a far more valuable tale to tell, but even her story would be a partial one. To get a fuller picture you would need to choose a wider range of people: perhaps one of the local shopkeepers, someone from one of the helping professions, someone of Italian or German descent, and a few younger people who were children at the time.

*No oral history project can aim for a statistically accurate sample of the population, but even in small projects you should ensure that the people you choose to interview are representative of a range of views.*

With contemporary projects, similar procedures apply. If you wanted to investigate how people in your area used their back yards there would be little point in interviewing people who have no land around their homes. However, having excluded this group, you should ensure that the group that you do select to interview includes the major ethnic groups in your area, young families and retirees, people living in shared households, single-parent families etc. At some time during the project you may also decide to go and talk to the person at your local council responsible for enforcing the relevant by-laws restricting activities on private land as well.

**How reliable?** Having collected the information, how do we measure its reliability? Our interviewees give us their understanding of the event, which we asked them to discuss; an understanding which is influenced by the fallibility of their memory, their subsequent experiences, and changes in their circumstances and attitudes. It will also be influenced by the political and social environment in which the interview took place and by the relationship between interviewer and interviewee.

Memory certainly is fallible, but memory loss is by no means uniform. Oral historians take comfort from the fact that the first discarding of information is the most dramatic. The material that does make the transition from the short- to the long-term memory remains intact for a very long time indeed. However, not everything makes this transition. We tend to remember things which seem important to us at the time, discarding much which may later be of greater importance. There is also a tendency to favour pleasant memories and repress the painful, and to recall incidents without being able to remember the emotions which accompanied them. That is why our grandparents always assure us that the summers were warmer, the food was tastier and the children always modest and respectful when they were young. However, with careful questioning, based on detailed preparation, the interviewer can compensate for this tendency to look at everything with a rosy glow.

Similar techniques are needed to control for the influence of later experiences on oral testimony. In this sense your interview, like any other source, needs to be treated critically and measured against other information to assess its validity. A born-again conservative may well place a different construction upon the politics of his student years than would a fellow student who has continued to be involved in radical causes. A worker who has been exposed to Marxist ideas will interpret his situation quite differently from one who has had no such exposure. No evidence is completely objective, and oral testimony is certainly no exception. You need to understand how the testimony has been constructed in order to assess both its validity and its significance.

*Most importantly, be aware that interviewing is a two-way process, and be prepared to both control and evaluate your influence on the resulting testimony.*

There is a further complication in this process for, unlike written sources, oral evidence is also actively constructed by the researcher. Your relationship with the interviewee and the direction of your questions both influence the answers which you receive. Most interviewees are eager to please. They will provide the information they think you want to hear and draw back from areas where they sense you are uncomfortable. Many are unlikely to challenge your preconceived view of the past. Hence it is important not to let your view intrude. Come well-prepared with information, but be careful not to let your interpretations structure the interview. Take care in your choice of subjects not to put yourself in a situation where your relationship with the interviewee is going to make discussing large areas of relevant material difficult or impossible.

**Be prepared.** With these warnings in mind are we now ready then to set out? Unfortunately not. The interview is only one small part in the research process and its success depends on your being carefully prepared. The people you are going to interview will all have limited time. Preparation will ensure that you make best use of the time they have available.

Interviewing is no substitute for reading. Before you begin to ask questions, you need to have worked your way through the written source material. You need this familiarity in order to make sense of what your interviewee has to say. It will also help you determine the questions you are going to ask. If, for example, you were investigating the experiences of Australian prisoners-of-war during the Second World War, you would need to read some general texts to find out who was captured and why. You would also have to become familiar with the principal camps, perhaps some of the leading 'personalities' within those camps, and the conditions which they endured. Only with the basic names, dates and places fixed in your mind can you present yourself to your subject.

You need also to make some practical preparations. Use your reading to prepare an interview outline. A casual, unstructured conversation may seem pleasant, but it is not an efficient way to use the time available and may not produce much of the information you set out to obtain. At the other extreme a rigid questionnaire approach may exclude relevant material which you have not been able to anticipate. A guide, from which you feel free to diverge to pursue relevant material, is often the best compromise. It ensures that you are never at a loss for your next question and, if you use it over a range of interviews, will give consistency to the basic material which you collect.

You would find it useful to do a pilot interview to find out the most useful questions.

The Interview Record (Figure 3.4) will help you to prepare for and record the interview.

The Informant Profile (Figure 3.5) is a form you could adapt for your own use to record the details of the person you are interviewing. As you can see, it is a very comprehensive form, and you probably will only need a portion of it for your particular purposes. For example, you may not need all the family history material and all the employment details, but you must decide this for yourself. This form is for your own records, so you should fill it in *before* and *after* the interview when you have the appropriate information, not during the interview.

Figure 3.4   Interview record

## Interview record

Name of interviewer: _____

Name of interviewee: _____

Date and place of interview: _____

Relevant background information on interviewee:

_____

_____

_____

_____

No. of tapes for this interview: _____

| Tape index no. | Questions | Answers |
|---|---|---|
| | | |
| | | |
| | | |

Evaluation of interview:

_____

_____

_____

_____

Summary of interview:

_____

_____

_____

_____

This form was based on one in *Oral History: A Handbook*, by Louise Douglas, Alan Roberts and Ruth Thompson (Allen & Unwin, 1988)

Figure 3.5   Informant profile

| Informant Profile |
| --- |

1 _____    _____    _____
        Title                       Surname                          First name(s)

_____
Maiden name (if applicable)

2  Name and birthdates of brothers and sisters

   i)  _____     _____

  ii)  _____     _____

 iii)  _____     _____

 iv)  _____     _____

  v)  _____     _____

 vi)  _____     _____

3  Mother's first name(s) _____

   Mother's maiden name _____

   Date of birth _____     Place of birth _____

   Date of marriage _____     Place of marriage _____

   Date of death _____     Place of death _____

   Cause of death _____

   Occupation(s) before marriage _____

   _____

   Occupation(s) after marriage _____

   _____

4  Father's first name(s) _____

   Father's surname _____

   Date of birth _____     Place of birth _____

   Date of marriage _____     Place of marriage _____

   Date of death _____     Place of death _____

   Cause of death _____

*continued*

Occupation(s) before marriage _____

_____

Occupation(s) after marriage _____

_____

5  Religion of:

Mother _____

Father _____

Informant _____

6  Marital status _____     Place of marriage _____

Name of spouse_____     Religion _____

Occupation of spouse _____

7  Name and birthdates of children

   i)  _____     _____

   ii)  _____     _____

   iii)  _____     _____

   iv)  _____     _____

   v)  _____     _____

   vi)  _____     _____

8  Locality(ies) in which interviewee grew up (please specify years in each place)

_____

_____

_____

9  Names of educational institutions and years attended

Pre-school     _____     _____

Primary     _____     _____

             _____     _____

*continued overleaf*

Secondary _____    _____

_____    _____

Tertiary _____    _____

_____    _____

10  Employment history

| Year | Employer's name and address | Income | Duties |
|------|------------------------------|--------|--------|
| ____ | _____ | _____ | _____ |
| ____ | _____ | _____ | _____ |
| ____ | _____ | _____ | _____ |
| ____ | _____ | _____ | _____ |
| ____ | _____ | _____ | _____ |
| ____ | _____ | _____ | _____ |
| ____ | _____ | _____ | _____ |

11  Accommodation (from birth to present)

| Year | Location | Type of dwelling | Owned/rented private/govt | Head of household |
|------|----------|------------------|---------------------------|-------------------|
| ____ | _____ | _____ | _____ | _____ |
| ____ | _____ | _____ | _____ | _____ |
| ____ | _____ | _____ | _____ | _____ |
| ____ | _____ | _____ | _____ | _____ |
| ____ | _____ | _____ | _____ | _____ |

12  Name of interviewer _____

Address _____    Postcode _____

Date of interview _____    No. of tapes _____

Source: Douglas L., Roberts A and Thompson R. *Oral History: A Handbook*, Allen & Unwin Pty Ltd, North Sydney 1988. pp 79-82.

Finally, you need to check your technology. Your memory, too, is fallible so, except for short, fact-finding interviews, you should always tape your material. Before you set out make sure your tape recorder is working and that if it runs on batteries, they are fresh. Take plenty of clean tape — one or two cassettes. A second test just before the interview begins is always a wise procedure as well.

## What to ask and how to ask it?

And so you are on the doorstep, tape recorder in hand. Where do we go from here? Living, breathing sources are not as simple to deal with as written ones. Before you turn on the tape recorder, try and set your interviewee at ease. Find a comfortable place for both of you to sit, free of outside interference, but handy to a power point for the tape recorder, if you need an electric power supply. Talk a little about your project and then outline your interview plan so that your interviewee knows what to expect. Explain the tape recorder, and record an identification of the interview. This reduces some of the fear of technology and means that you can check that everything is working before you begin. When you both feel comfortable then you are ready to begin.

Start with the basic identifying questions. As you both relax you can move on to more complex material. If you feel comfortable taking notes, do

so, but remember the most important thing is to listen to what your interviewee is saying so that your next question is an appropriate one. Follow up interesting material even if it is offered a little out of sequence. If your interviewee seems to be wandering, don't intervene too abruptly. Wait for an appropriate time and then ask a question which takes the focus back to the point which you wanted to explore. Never engage in argument, although you can try to clarify a seeming inaccuracy by more careful questioning. If your interviewee continues to offer material which you know to be wrong, there is nothing to be achieved by openly challenging it. It is, after all, your interviewee's perception of events which you are seeking to record, not your own.

Begin each new subject with an open-ended question, following up the interesting points which arise with a series of more specific enquiries. Avoid questions which require only a 'yes' or 'no' answer, and any framed in terms of your preconceptions. Questions which invite specific answers are more useful that those which can be answered with generalities.

If you were asking your grandmother about her early years at school you might begin with some very specific questions about when and where she went to school, before moving into some more general enquiries.

Introductory questions:
Where did you first go to school?
What year would that have been?
How many children were there?

Broad opening questions:
What do you remember about those early years?

Follow-up questions:
What subjects did you study?
What games did you play?
What punishments were used?

Specific follow-up questions:
You mentioned the cane; how often was it used?
Did girls get the cane as well as boys?
Tell me about the time you were punished this way?
How did you feel then?

Questions like these give your interviewee the freedom to actively contribute to the discussion and open up areas of interest, while allowing you to focus your area of interest and get more specific information where this is required.

To check the effectiveness of open versus closed questions, try this exercise.

Pretend you are the interviewee and answer the questions listed above from your own experience. Now do the same thing with this series of questions:

You began school in. . . ?

That was . . . school, wasn't it?

Did it have a lot of pupils?

I suppose you were pretty scared?

Did you spend most of your time doing reading and arithmetic?

We had seasons, hopping, marbles, skipping etc.

Was it the same thing in your day?

I suppose the teachers were very strict?

The cane was used all the time, I expect?

I think that kind of punishment was the making of us.

Don't you agree?

Now compare your answers to the two sets of questions. Which produced the most useful information? Which made you feel valued as an interviewee?

Interviewing is as much about *responding to feelings* as it is about responding to information. Don't rush in to fill silences with further questions. Sometimes a nod of the head or an encouraging smile will produce a rush of valuable information. While you should not seek to pry into sensitive areas, if your interviewee seems to be getting upset, accept the validity of these feelings and work through them rather than quickly shying away and leaving them feeling uncomfortable. Show a genuine interest in the material which is being offered and explain its value to your project at regular points in the process so that your interviewee is reassured that what they have to offer is indeed of value. Finally, keep an eye on the time so that you can round the interview off neatly rather than having it end with a rush when the tape comes to an end.

Remember too, that when the tape finishes, the interview does not. Take time to wind down with your interviewee. Thank them for the information which they have given and talk a little about how you see it being put to use. Check any points that you have not fully understood. Reassure them about the confidentiality of the material which they have shared.

## Group interviews

Everything in the preceding section on individual interviews applies to group interviews, but remember these do place special demands on the interviewer.

You would consider using a group interview:

- for convenience if this is the only time, say, a family or members of a team can see you;

TOO MANY IN A GROUP MAKES AN INTERVIEW IMPOSSIBLE TO CONTROL

- if you want to get various views on an issue but haven't the time to interview individuals.

The main problem with a group interview is keeping track of the responses, so keep the numbers small — nothing over ten.

### Special points about group interviews

- At the interview draw a diagram of the table with each person's name and position noted. This will help you to identify the participants during the interview and later when you analyse the information.
- You may need more sophisticated taping equipment with directional microphones for this type of interview. Try out your equipment on a similar-sized group of your friends first. Make sure everyone at the interview can be heard on your tape by an initial test. Nothing is worse, after all this effort, than to have a garbled, noisy interview.
- Members of the group will need to identify themselves before they speak, otherwise you will not be able to identify participants for transcription and analysis.
- A group interview is more difficult to manage and to keep focused on your questions. You will have to intervene in the discussion to make sure your questions are answered. Slow down the discussion, if necessary.

- It is important that you fill in your interview record very carefully for group interviews so that you can access the taped material at the right points for your research project.

## How to transcribe and summarise your tapes

The information which you have collected is raw data. Now you need to decide just how you can use it in your project. The first step, wherever possible, is to have your tape transcribed. This gives you your material in a much more accessible form and allows you to send a copy to your interviewee for checks and amendments. It is a time-consuming process, as the interview needs to be transcribed in full, particularly if it is to be kept as any kind of permanent record.

If you cannot afford to have your tapes transcribed, you should listen to them carefully, summarising their principal points so that you will be able to access them quickly for future use. Your 'Interview Record' form will be of great assistance here. If you can't make a full transcript, your interview on tape can be adapted to a modified written form if you follow a few simple procedures:

- Listen to the interview a couple of times from beginning to end and get a general feel for the information being given.
- From this you should be able to write a brief summary of the interview.
- Armed with your interview questions and any notes you may have taken during the course of the interview, listen to the interview. Make a note of the response you got to each question you asked. You may need to stop the recorder frequently so that you can be as accurate as possible.

You may even want to write down the exact words that your interviewee used.

Recording this on paper can be done in a number of ways, depending on your requirements. If you want to keep several interviews on permanent record, this might best be done by devising a standard 'Interview Record' form, with details of the interview at the top, and below that, space for the recording of questions on one side of the paper and the answers next to them. See Figure 3.4.

You might be just as content with a less formal approach where only those questions of particular relevance to you are recorded, rather than the entire interview. Be sure, however, to be precise about your requirements and be as accurate as possible. You are, after all, using other people's words and thoughts, so you owe it to them to be careful.

When recording your interview in writing, remember to include details of the interview such as the date, place, duration, and any other relevant matters. Provide a general summary at the beginning so anyone can see at a glance the subject of the interview. Decide how detailed your written recording needs to be and proceed with your work from that view.

Remember, be as accurate as possible. If you are recording the exact words of your subject, identify them in some clear way; for example, write them in a different colour.

## How to check your interview for validity

Once you have your written transcript or summary, you need to check it further for validity. Check it against other external evidence. Then look for evidence of internal inconsistency or implausibility. Follow up any points where you find that you need more information. Try to assess the impact of the relationship between you and your interviewee on the material produced and make a note at any point where you feel this has had an impact on the answers provided.

Finally, remember a thank-you note or telephone call to your interviewee thanking them for their co-operation.

With these checks all complete you have in hand the oral evidence you were seeking when your research began. You know its strengths and its weaknesses and the reliability of the source from which it came. Go ahead and use it with confidence!

## How to analyse the results of your interview

Having collected your oral material how do you then find out what it has to tell you?

Your first step should be to return to your original questions. Why did you undertake the interviews? What answers did you think they would provide that could not be found elsewhere? Look at your notes or transcripts. What do they tell you about your initial questions? Organise the material under these original headings being sure to distinguish between when you are quoting directly from the interview and when you are adding impressions or conclusions of your own.

Now check the transcripts for material that you did not anticipate. Do they cast new light on the subject you were investigating or suggest alternative ways of looking at your initial research question? When this material is relevant you should incorporate it into your summary of results, adding new headings when necessary to augment your original list.

If you interviewed several people you should go on to compare your findings from each. Are similar answers being given to the original series of questions or do they vary? Can these variations be related to the range of people you interviewed? Do women see a given situation differently from men, for example? Do people recalling their childhood remember a given event differently from those who were adult at the time? How does social class or ethnic background affect the responses which you have collected? Here it may be useful to construct a hypothesis as to how you would expect such features to influence the evidence collected. You could then test it on your series of interviews. Are there any consistent patterns which seem to emerge?

Now check your data against other sources which examine a similar problem or time period. To what extent does your material confirm what other people have found? When does it differ? What explanations can you put forward for such differences as do emerge? How could your data be used to interpret an accepted view?

Your answers to this series of questions will provide the basis for your report. Whether your interviews are central or peripheral to your research project you need to clearly understand their significance for the project as a whole. What have you found that confirms existing views? What have you found that is new? What qualifications do you need to place on the validity of your material? What further research questions does it suggest for anyone who would like to investigate the subject further?

Finally, when your report is completed, don't discard the material on which it is based. Your school library may like to keep your tapes for others to refer to in the future. If your report is on a historical subject perhaps your local historical society would be interested. In conducting your research you have also created evidence for future scholars, so treat it with care.

## The importance of oral history

As we have mentioned, interviews are especially useful research tools for Australians with a strong oral tradition who are not well-represented in written sources, especially women, children, Aborigines and Australians of different ethnic backgrounds.

This means that if the experience of most Australians is to be included in research studies, oral history is a vital research tool. An early book which showed the value of oral history in documenting the experience of post-war immigrants was Morag Loh's book, *The Immigrants*, which was based on interviews with post-war immigrants who settled in Melbourne. A more recent study of immigrants who worked on the Snowy River Scheme (Margaret Unger, *Voices from the Snowy*, NSW University Press, 1989) has shown the range of experience of new migrants coming to a remote area. Recently the Aborigines of Victoria told their history in *Living Aboriginal History of Victoria* (CUP, 1991). If you are to undertake similar interview projects, you will need to be sure that you have the necessary background, contacts and language skills. An understanding of different traditions can be gained through background reading; help with translation may be arranged through ethnic community organisations if you do not speak the language of your informant. Aboriginal oral history and interviews are also best undertaken in consultation with Aboriginal organisations. Louise Douglas, Alan Roberts and Ruth Thompson's book *Oral History: a handbook* has a helpful guide to interviewing Aborigines on pages 74-76 .

# (iv) Participant observation

Another important tool for your research project has been adapted from the work of anthropologists: participant observation. The in-depth interview and the case study can also be included under this heading. All rely on careful observation of people and groups. However, if observation of people is used as your research method, you must be prepared to have a more interactive approach than with surveys and to see issues through other people's eyes.

Given the multicultural nature of Australian society, this type of research tool could be one of the most valuable to use, as it enables the researcher to develop an understanding of other cultures. This research tool is useful to study not only those of different ethnic backgrounds, but also for any group which you want to find out more about, for example, workers in a factory.

Participant observation enables you to observe what *actually* happens, rather than what people *say* happens. Quite often those who have answered your questionnaires tell you what they think would be the 'right' answer. They don't always want to own up to what they really think or do. Observation can also help you discover the unwritten rules or norms of people's behaviour. Take an example of something as simple as watching a tennis match on television. Even in this removed 'observation' role you can note that the crowd claps or refrains from clapping in certain situations, e.g. when a player loses a point because of a mistake, and that the players themselves also have an unwritten code of behaviour that can be documented. Watching your own family at a meal can also reveal unwritten codes of behaviour. Who washes the dishes? Who contributes to the conversation? By writing down what actually happens at a family meal you can learn about gender roles and relationships in the family.

This type of observation involves participation. You can't pretend to be detached; you are now part of the scene. This means that you are going to be more involved; your research will be more of an experience and involvement. This degree of involvement can vary; you can join a group and observe a situation of which you are a part, for instance a scout troop, or you can observe without taking a more active role, for example, attending a community meeting.

There are problems with observation to take into account:
- Being accepted by the group you wish to observe can sometimes be a problem. There is room for much misunderstanding here, so make sure that your approach is careful.
- Participant observation may be covert or overt. 'In *Covert Participant Observation* those being observed do not know that you are studying them; they think that you are an ordinary member of the group. This

raises the moral or ethical problem of whether it is acceptable to observe people in this way. In *Overt Participant Observation* the participants know they are being observed and this might cause them to act differently.' (Lynn Williams, *Finding Out About Society*, p. 34.)

- What is collected and how it is interpreted depends on the researcher's values. It is important to talk with the people who are involved in the events and actions being observed, and understand their interpretations and understandings.

## Research steps

**Step 1. Access to the group.** This a more difficult problem in participant observation than in survey research where only written and structured responses are required. There could be resistance from a group to a request from a researcher to observe. As usual, it is easier, but less rewarding from a research point of view, to approach a group that you know well. A contact who could introduce you, or a carefully worded letter of explanation about the purposes of your research would be the best way to join a group where you are not known.

It is important to realise before you choose participant observation as a research tool that getting into a group and having your research role accepted can be the most difficult part. If you are undertaking classroom observation, or attending a public meeting, access will obviously be much simpler.

Another important planning consideration with participant observation research is to make sure you have an adequate time span. Some ETHNOGRAPHIC RESEARCHERS spend months or even years studying their group. For most secondary students only a relatively short time span will be possible, but it must be long enough for you to understand the norms of the group you are studying.

**Step 2. Recording information.** Again this is more difficult in participant observation than in survey research. You need to be very clear about what you are looking for before you start. For example, in a classroom observation of a maths lesson your research interests may be to note the different reactions of boys and girls to the lesson and also of the time the teacher gives to members of each group. As you are observing an event in time, you cannot later think of a question and go back to the same class. You will need a record sheet for most participant observation sessions. A record sheet for the maths lesson could be as in Figure 3.6.

If you are attending a public meeting and want to record the interaction of those attending, you would prepare a grid similar to that in Figure 3.7.

Recording participant observation sessions requires a good memory. If you are recording a meeting you will need to take notes that can be written

Figure 3.6  Participant observation session

| Participant Observation Session | | |
|---|---|---|
| Date of observation: _____ | | |
| Place of observation: _____ | | |
| Research question: What are the different experiences of male and female students in a maths lesson? | | |

| | male | female |
|---|---|---|
| Teacher | ✓ | |
| No. of students | 16 | 7 |
| Questions asked by students | 3 | 5 |
| No. of problems completed | 6 | 6 |
| Time spent by teachers with students | 15 mins | 10 mins |

up later. A diary recording your participation would be useful if you are having a number of meetings with your group.

**Step 3. Analysing results.** As with surveys, some tables and graphs can be used to present research material, but generally with participant observation your analysis will be descriptive. On the basis of your records and diaries you will need to write an *analysis* that makes general points about the groups you observed and give examples.

As always this analysis must be focused around your research questions. To go back to the maths class study, your analysis would include the number of questions asked by boys compared with those asked by girls, and then a comparison of the number of problems completed by each gender group. Interaction between the teacher and boys and girls in the class would be more descriptive with examples given to show the different questions asked by each sex and differences in the teacher's response.

After summing up your findings it is important that you *record your experience* of being an observer. Did your presence influence the way the teacher and students interacted? Did you identify more with your own sex

Figure 3.7    Evaluation of meeting participation

| Participant | No. of questions asked | Numbers of interventions and time | Attitude to other participants | Comments on other involvement | Overall rating of contribution |
|---|---|---|---|---|---|
| Jean C | | | | | |
| George M | | | | | |
| Ann Y | | | | | |
| etc. | | | | | |
| | | | | | |
| | | | | | |
| | | | | | |
| | | | | | |
| | | | | | |
| | | | | | |
| | | | | | |

and understand their problems better? Asking such questions will make you aware of how important your opinions and experience are in influencing research outcomes — an important aspect of participant observation research.

# (v) Material culture and visual resources

The image of research projects is often associated with written reports, surveys and statistical analysis. Increasingly, social scientists are aware of the value of the every-day records of family life. These include diaries, photographs, household items and craftwork. It can also cover evidence of the built environment expressed in buildings, streets, and the way suburbs and towns have developed. These are important sources of evidence about the way people relate to one another and construct individual and community relationships.

The images people create of themselves individually and in communities can be studied in part by borrowing some of the approaches of ANTHROPOLOGISTS, especially their emphasis on collecting and interpreting MATERIAL CULTURE — the buildings and objects used in every-day life.

You may ask 'why bother with objects in researching the past when so much of our history has been written down?' As has been mentioned before, the problem is that the written documents we find so informative — such as diaries, letters, government reports and the like — were written by people who were educated, literate, and who had the time to write; this means they are a very selective source. Compulsory schooling occurred in most states of Australia in the 1870s, but even so, we cannot assume that because children were all schooled, they could read and write. Thus large sectors of the population are not well represented by written records, in particular, Aborigines and people of other ethnic backgrounds. Drawing on the world around you for your research project means that the 'invisible' people — women, children, the elderly, and the other population groups mentioned above, who are under-represented in many research projects — assume a place more in proportion to their numbers in the population.

This section focuses on the way buildings and streetscapes, as well as material culture and photographs, can be used in your research project and can be used in conjunction with written records and oral history.

### Buildings and streetscapes — what can be observed in the built environment?

Begin with the Australian suburban house or flat, but not just the outside; examine the inside. Domestic interiors are a marvellous source of information on family interactions, as they reflect the very essence of domestic life and labour. Where are the private and communal areas of a house? Is the dining area a more important focus for family gatherings than the television

Figure 3.8 Comparing house plans identifies family relationships

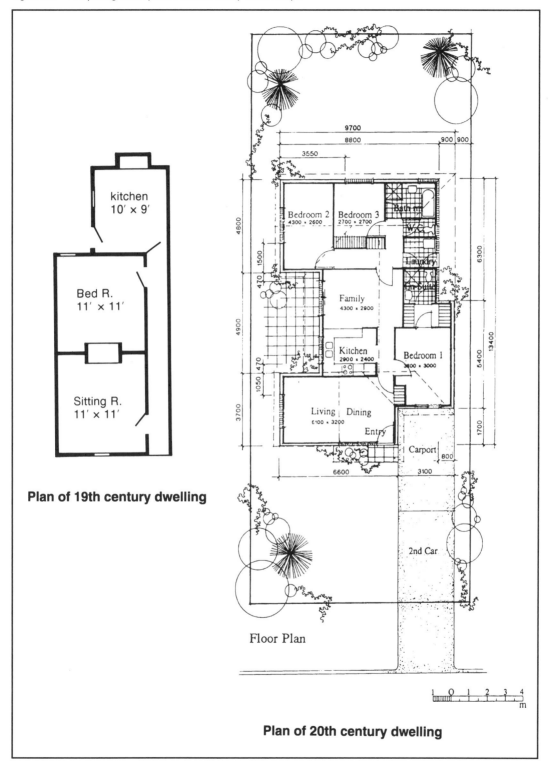

**Plan of 19th century dwelling**

kitchen
10′ × 9′

Bed R.
11′ × 11′

Sitting R.
11′ × 11′

Floor Plan

Bedroom 2
4300 × 2600

Bedroom 3
2700 × 2700

Bath m

w.c.

Laundry

Family
4300 × 2900

Kitchen
2900 × 2400

Bedroom 1
3400 × 3000

Living    Dining
6100 × 3200

Entry

Carport

2nd Car

**Plan of 20th century dwelling**

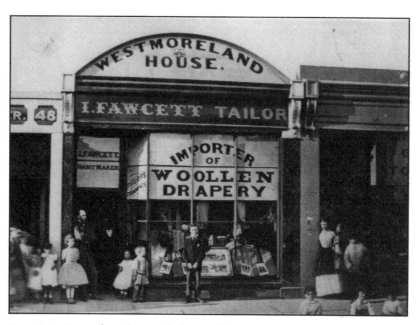

Figure 3.9  'Face to face' shopping before World War II

area? How are parents' areas separated from children's areas? What do these separations indicate about the interaction of parents and children? Does the house have areas where the women are dominant, and other areas where the males assert their authority? If you are doing a historical study for your research project, comparing interior layouts of houses of different periods will provide evidence of changes in family relationships. (See Figure 3.8.)

Interiors of industrial and commercial buildings are also important, and are evidence of relationships in the workplace and with customers. The two-storey shop, characteristic of Australian urban main streets until the Second World War, was based on a relatively small retail space where customers were served face-to-face. The owner or manager's family lived above or behind the shop and was part of the surrounding community. Compare this with the modern supermarket or hypermarket, where the only human interaction is the frenetic activity at checkout points.

The organisation of space within an office can also yield information about the way people interact, and the role of gender and power. The large open-plan office can be studied for the way space is allocated and how this is related to tasks and job hierarchies. Sometimes those with the more important tasks for the functioning of the office get the smallest and worst locations, while those with managerial functions have more space in better locations. Industrial workplaces also provide evidence of power relation-ships in the way work and space is organised, while gender differences are often still evident in the allocation of jobs. Your own school, if looked at as a place of work, can also be a source of information if you analyse the way

Figure 3.10 The changing streetscape of Victoria Street, North Melbourne

(a) 1880s

*La Trobe Collection, State Library of Victoria*

(b) 1970s

Figure 3.11  Street survey — data collection form — social and architectural

| Building address | Building type<br>R – Residential<br>C – Commercial<br>I – Institutional<br>M – Manufacturing | Estimated age | Architectural style | Building materials | Changes in structure and use | Social rating – economic<br>High<br>Medium<br>Low |
|---|---|---|---|---|---|---|
| | | | | | | |

that space is allocated between different teaching areas, and between teachers, students and support staff.

Buildings and streetscapes provide another perspective. Relationships between work, shopping, leisure and home, as well as the social status of communities can be analysed through streetscapes. The layers of change, always evident in the built environment, can be studied through a careful analysis of a street. (Also read 'The built environment' on pp. 102-4.)

**How to study the built environment.** Studying the built environment requires skills of observation. Shane Cahill and David Paul in 'The eyes have it — an observational approach' have spelled out the following observation hierarchy which can be used for buildings and streetscapes. (*Past Continuous*, Judy MacKinolty (ed.), p. 36.)

*Simple observation:* looking and noticing things that are there.
*Recognition:* identifying the main characteristics.
*Explanation:* accounting for main characteristics. This will require some framework of knowledge of the local area.
*Analysis:* placing observations in a framework of change over time.
*Evaluation:* developing judgements about the significance of the material.

As usual, you will need to record your observations so that they are in a usable form for analysis and make the maximum contribution to your research project. The form in Figure 3.11 is a suggested way of collating information for a streetscape survey with the objective of studying the present and past mix of residential, commercial and industrial uses, and changing social status. Remember, the urban environment is always changing; demolition, alteration, new people moving in, different uses for buildings are all common in any established Australian town or suburb. This is what makes them such excellent material for your research project.

The quality of your observation will be helped by your preparation, especially background reading and reference to plans and maps. It is not always easy to judge the age of buildings and categorise architectural styles, and you will need to consult a reference such as Robin Boyd's *Australia's Home*, which is a useful introduction to domestic architecture. Some commercial buildings will have the date of their construction on the parapet and institutional buildings will often have foundation stones. Interviewing residents will often help you with information on dating, what the building looked like in the past, and its uses over time.

If you want to use your streetscape study to do a research project focused on environmental issues rather than issues of social and urban change, a form based on Figure 3.12 could be used.

Figure 3.12  Street survey — data collection form — environmental

## Street survey – data collection form – environmental

| | Streetscape factor | Observation | Aesthetic rating | | | Reason for rating |
|---|---|---|---|---|---|---|
| | | | High | Medium | Low | |
| 1 | Slope of land | | | | | |
| 2 | Waterways | | | | | |
| 3 | Number of buildings | | | | | |
| 4 | Use of buildings | | | | | |
| 5 | Age of buildings | | | | | |
| 6 | Height of buildings | | | | | |
| 7 | Building materials | | | | | |
| 8 | Colour of buildings | | | | | |
| 9 | Roof materials | | | | | |
| 10 | Condition of buildings | | | | | |
| 11 | Block size     Width     Depth | | | | | |
| 12 | Style of fencing | | | | | |
| 13 | Fencing materials | | | | | |
| 14 | Type of garden | | | | | |
| 15 | Care of garden | | | | | |
| 16 | Care of naturestrip | | | | | |
| 17 | Street trees     Number     Type | | | | | |
| 18 | Width of road | | | | | |
| 19 | Condition of road | | | | | |
| 20 | Type of kerbing | | | | | |
| 21 | Public transport | | | | | |
| 22 | Traffic management | | | | | |
| 23 | Number of parking spaces | | | | | |
| 24 | Number of cars parked | | | | | |
| 25 | Number of street signs | | | | | |
| 26 | Number of power poles | | | | | |
| 27 | Advertising     Amount     Type | | | | | |
| 28 | Litter     Amount     Type | | | | | |
| 29 | Open space     Amount     Type | | | | | |
| 30 | Public facilities     Amount     Type | | | | | |

## Artefacts: Objects as pathways into the past

The study of ARTEFACTS or material culture enables us to reconstruct how an object originated, functioned and continues to function today. The study of every-day objects yields an understanding of our culture and traditions, as they enable a reconstruction of the life-styles of especially families, ethnic groups and communities.

The study of objects or artefacts can shed light on groups who were previously silent in history or who were written about, but not by their own people. Archaeologists, art historians and museum curators have always studied artefacts or material culture. It is only recently that this study is becoming a recognised area of study within other social science disciplines in Australia.

The advantage of a study of material culture is its accessibility. If your research project is concerned with domestic work, a historical study of the needlework undertaken by women in a household can further the understanding of gender roles, family relationships and the contributions of paid and unpaid work to the domestic economy. If you were able to collect needlework done by mothers, grandmothers and great-grandmothers, you would be able to compare the changing nature of women's domestic work, the influence of technology such as the introduction of the sewing machine, and the influence of mass-produced clothing and household linen.

Similar studies can be undertaken using ordinary kitchen equipment, or tools from the garage or garden. Many museums now have displays of ordinary household artefacts which they combine with transcripts of oral interviews and pictorial material to explore domestic experience at different time periods. The Powerhouse Museum in Sydney has several such displays.

The use of artefacts is of particular value in studying households and communities of different ethnic backgrounds. The relationship of a family to its country of settlement, and the significance of past cultural traditions, can be interpreted from domestic records, not only those made or acquired in Australia, but those chosen to be brought by the original settlers.

Material objects then, are a complex cultural phenomenon that express family and community values. Most are of 'sentimental' rather than monetary value, and are often passed from generation to generation or from friend to friend. By understanding how they were made, used and passed on, you will be able to understand, or begin to understand, how people responded to the circumstances of their lives. (See Diane Bell, *Generations*.)

The study of artefacts should not be confined to the domestic and family sphere. Such a study is also relevant to non-domestic workplaces. A study of farm equipment can lead to understandings, not only of changing technology, but also of changing work practices and relationships on the farm. The work of other members of the family and the farm labourer may not be as necessary with new equipment. This, in turn, will have an impact on the farmer's self-image, as well as on domestic relationships and on the economy and social life of the local community.

**Selection criteria.** Your choice of objects will be governed by your research objectives. It is important to choose objects which you are sure you can identify and document. Interviews will be important in establishing the significance of the object, the extent and way in which it has been handed on, the way or ways in which it has functioned and been adapted. Photographs are also an important source of information on how an object has been used and perceived.

**How do we examine objects?** Firstly, the object you have located must be described. The description should be related to what can be observed in the object itself. Begin with the largest, most comprehensive observation and progress to the more particular details. Do not make any assumptions here, just describe what you see. You will need to measure and record the physical size of the object and perhaps weigh it, then describe the materials it is made from. Next, describe the ways the object has been put together. For example, for a wooden box, you would describe the types of joins used. Describe any decorative designs or colours, and whether the object is two- or three-dimensional. For example, the box may have the maker's or retailer's label on the inside, such as 'Foy and Gibson'. (Refer to J. D. Prown, 'Mind in Matter: An Introduction to Material Culture Theory and Method' in R. B. St. George, *Material Life in America 1600-1860*, Boston, Northeastern University Press, 1988, pp. 24-6.)

The second stage of analysis moves from the object itself to the way you experience the object. Here you need to imagine what it would be like to use the object. Then, from your own knowledge of the physical world, start to make DEDUCTIONS about how the object may have been used. Your deductions should be commonsensical. For example, you may deduce that the wooden box is too large for keeping small items, such as jewellery, so perhaps it was used for small tools of some type. Then consider your emotional response to the object. How does this object make you feel? Is it familiar to you? Is it strange? Is it attractive? Does it smell? This is all useful information contributing to the overall picture you are building up.

The third stage of analysis is SPECULATION, that is, creative imagining. Use your skills of empathy. After reviewing what you have recorded so far in the previous two stages, it is now time to develop theories that may explain the object and its uses. These ideas should then be tested through scholarly investigation of other external evidence, which is the fourth stage — VALIDATION.

You will need to develop sources of other evidence to prove or disprove your theories. For example, in order to identify the large wooden box, you might consult the Foy and Gibson catalogues in the State Library of

Figure 3.13 Artefacts data sheet

## Artefacts data sheet

Name of object: _____

Date of period used: _____

Where used: _____

Materials of manufacture: _____

_____

_____

Dimensions: _____

_____

_____

Description: _____

_____

_____

_____

_____

History: _____

_____

_____

_____

_____

_____

_____

_____

_____

Victoria. (Foy and Gibson was a large retail emporium in Melbourne earlier this century.) In Sydney, you could consult the Powerhouse Museum for their help. What other sources could you use to identify the box?

You will need to move back and forth through these different stages of analysis to gain maximum information about the object, and you may be surprised at just how much knowledge about an object you may finish with. Your analysis will be easier if you have carefully documented the objects selected for your research study. (See Figure 3.13.)

### Interpreting an object using oral history.

Your grandmother may have crocheted doilies or embroidered a tablecloth many years ago. You could start to investigate these historical artefacts by, firstly, asking yourself questions about them and then asking her questions to verify your ideas and impressions. Here are some possible questions:

When did you make this item?
Why did you make it?
What purpose or function did it have?
How often did you use it?
Was it for special occasions or for every-day use?
What were the special occasions?
How long did it take you to make it?
Did you use a pattern for it or did you design it yourself?
Who taught you to crochet/sew?
How old were you when you learnt?
Did you learn sewing at school?
How often did you do this work?
What time of day did you do it?
How did you feel about it? Did you like it or hate it?
Who else did this type of craft?

Through the answers to these questions you will build up a picture of not just the object's purpose and function, but many other aspects as well. These could be:

- your grandmother's social world at the time the object was made;
- role expectations and the treatment of girls and women;
- what girls were taught at school at that time;
- ideas of appropriate behaviour for girls and women;
- the values and attitudes your grandmother held towards many things;
- the household routines, rituals, important occasions, the work done and methods used;
- their leisure pursuits;
- your grandmother's favourite activities; those she hated and why;
- the importance of family;
- the ways family life was lived, and what the concept meant to your grandmother;

Figure 3.14  Crocheted doily

- whether it has changed;
- household technology (electricity, appliances etc.) and much more.

In turn, this will give you insights and understanding of the ways your grandmother thinks, and her influence on your own parents. Through comparing this with your own experiences, you may gain new perspectives on your own situation. In this way, the study of an artefact of needlework or other artefacts can be personally enriching.

## Photographs: Windows in time

Pictorial evidence is an excellent source for the student researcher, again because it is readily available. Most families, since the days of the Box Brownie, have had a camera and kept photograph albums. Improvements in copying processes have meant that historical photographs are more widely available, while newspapers and magazines are a ready source of photographs and pictures, especially of public events. There are several areas of research for which photographs provide a useful research tool.

**Family history.** Photographs are a major record of family life, but a selective one. Photographs are usually taken of events that are deemed significant at the time. School classes, graduations, babies, weddings and holiday photographs abound. However, the photograph album will usually not record the family in moments of tragedy or at work in the home, office or factory. Family photographs are not complete records, but are culturally influenced representations of family life. It is this selectivity and the evidence it

Figure 3.15    Family history

Photographs have their own meanings. They can talk for themselves. They also have hidden meanings, locked away until we find appropriate keys. *(Professor Weston Bate in the introduction to* Curlew Country; Regionalism and Australia, *Deakin University, 1979.)*

provides of the changing views of family life that can make family albums a valuable source for your research project. In other words, the limited range of experience recorded by photographs is in one way a disadvantage. On the other hand, the reasons why particular events and subjects were chosen to be photographed and recorded can be an important part of your research project.

**The built environment.** Again, remember that the camera can lie! It is usually the houses that owners are proud of, or those that are considered worthy of interest by architects that are photographed. Even when more humble houses are pictured it is often to show how dilapidated and run-down they are. Enquiries into 'slum' housing are usually illustrated with photographs depicting the very worst housing.

Photographs of buildings and streets can be useful sources of evidence about urban changes, especially if you can collect photographs of the same building or street at different periods. In this way you can document changes in housing, shopping centres, transport, and the age or ethnicity of residents. You can take your own photographs, not just as illustration for your research project, but also as evidence to show different patterns of uses

Figure 3.16   Pictorial data sheet

## Pictorial data sheet

Picture

Subject matter: _____

_____

_____

Date photo taken: _____

Purpose: _____

_____

_____

_____

_____

Interpretation: _____

_____

_____

_____

_____

_____

of buildings and places. (Also read 'Buildings and streetscapes — what can be observed in the built environment' on pp. 90-6; see also Figure 3.9.)

**Multicultural Australia.** Photographs are a good source to document multi-cultural Australia. A recent study of Greek-Australians relied heavily on contemporary photographs portraying Greek-Australians from various social levels, occupations, ages, and in diverse settings — work and recreation, urban and rural — as well as tracing life from birth to death. Issues of interpretation and selection are again critical. In the case of the Greek-Australian study, a major aim of the project was to 'de-emphasise the existing stereotypes' of Greek-Australians as working-class urban residents perceived to be held by many in the community. This was done by showing the full range of life-styles in the Greek-Australian experience. (Refer to *New Responsibilities: documenting multicultural Australia*, Margaret Birtley and Patricia McQueen (eds), Museums Association of Australia/Library Council of Victoria, p.29.)

If you decide that pictures and photographs will be a useful tool for your research project, you will need to consider issues of interpretation, selection and collection. The pictorial evaluation and information sheet shown in Figure 3.16 will help you with an analysis of pictorial material, for example, what can be learned from the pose and setting of the photographs?

Dating historical photographs can be done by identifying the photographic process used or by asking a relative or resident. The photograph itself will provide some clues about the date on which it was taken through styles of dress, types of poses, or background objects and scenes. If you have borrowed photographs for your project, get reproductions made either at school or commercially as soon as possible and return the originals to their owners. Don't store even reproductions in plastic, as this can often cause damage. Photographs are best stored in manilla files and filed according to subject matter for easy reference when you come to the analysis and writing stage of your project.

As with the built environment and artefacts, photographs need keys, especially the key of oral history, to unlock all their meanings and the context of time and place. Written sources such as newspaper files also unlock the story of public events, while school and church records expand our knowledge of the pictorial record.

# PUTTING YOUR RESEARCH PROJECT TOGETHER

**4**

You have finished your reading and research. What do you do with all the information you have found out? How do you best analyse and present the data you have collected?

## Analysis

The interpretation and analysis of your research findings does not come at the end of the process. As you have been conducting your research you will have been asking yourself the meaning of what you have been finding out. Why did your survey throw up an unexpected result? What is the significance of a revealing interview? All along you have been *reflecting* on your research findings and their significance.

Now is the time to become more systematic about this reflection, and as you work through your readings and research findings, arrange them in organisational categories; search for the trends, relationships, themes and patterns that come through in your findings.

After you have done this first read-through, go back to your hypothesis and research questions. Have your findings been as expected? What has surprised you? Make notes of the responses and observations which you think have been most significant.

Having done this initial overview, you will then need to go back and examine your material in more detail. It is surprising how often researchers spend time finding vast amounts of information but don't spend the time on understanding and interpretation. Make sure you draw all you can out of the results of your hard work, especially with survey material.

No matter what the scale of your research project, it is important to explain your research findings in a clear and cogent way. Don't simply describe your research findings; the whole point of a research project is an *explanatory* one that goes beyond describing to analysing.

## Assessment

Before you do anything, focus your mind on the criteria that will be used to assess and evaluate your finished project. You can then ensure that your project meets this assessment criteria. There will be variations in the requirements for specific research projects, but most assessments and evaluations would include the following five criteria:

1. Originality
Does the project include original research material? Is the analysis thoughtful and based on your own conclusions?
2. Methodology
Have the most appropriate research tools been chosen for the subject? Has the research been carefully planned and carried out?
3. Substantial work
Is there evidence of substantial work in all sections of the project?
4. Integration
Does the research project hold together?
Do the conclusions follow on from the research findings?
5. Presentation
Have the aims and research findings of the project been effectively and clearly presented?
Check that your final written project includes all relevant components as detailed below.

# Research project checklist

1. Aim
Set out what your project intends to do clearly and concisely, defining terms and research questions.
2. Background
Give enough background to set the context: do not make this too long.
3. Methodology
Explain your research methodology and why you chose it.
4. Research results
Give results of your research. This might include graphs, quotes, figures or photographs.
5. Data analysis
Make an analysis of this research by pulling together your research results.
6. Evaluation
Have you answered your research questions?
7. Conclusion
Conclude by relating back to your introduction.
8. References
Reference your sources properly.
9. Appendixes
Add appendixes if appropriate.

Numbered appendixes may be added at the end of the text before the bibliography. It is a place to record material which is relevant, but which may not fit easily into the general text, e.g. the questionnaire you used, field maps you made, or statistics.

## Referencing your project

A primary requisite for any research is that you must acknowledge all the material you have consulted. Claiming or using other researchers' material as your own is an offence in academic pursuits. In fact it has a specific name — PLAGIARISM — and it is not an acceptable form of working.

There are essentially two ways or recording references: *notes* and a *bibliography*.

*Notes* are numbered references used throughout the text where you have quoted directly from another work, or where you have used someone else's ideas but written it differently; this is called paraphrasing. If you wish to add an explanation of other relevant material, a note can also be used. A number is placed in the text at the place where the note is relevant; the note itself is located either at the bottom of the page on which the number is located (footnote) or at the end of the chapter or the article (endnote). The acknowledgement must include the exact and complete source of the reference so that it can easily be found by someone who is looking for it, i.e. year of publication, title of book or article, author, publisher, page number. The exact order and recording of the notes should be in accordance with the standard and accepted forms of referencing for academic publishing. For example, corresponding to the numbers in your text:

*Footnotes:*
1. B. Graetz, and I. McAllister, *Dimensions of Australian Society*, Macmillan Co. of Australia, South Melbourne, 1988, p. 92.
2. P. Wilkie, 'For Friends at Home: some early views of Melbourne', *Latrobe Library Journal*, vol. 12, no. 46, 1991, p. 62.

A *bibliography* is a list arranged alphabetically by author af all sources of material used in your research project. Again, standard referencing methods must be used. For example:

*Bibliography*
Clark, C.M.H., *The Short History of Australia*, Penguin, Melbourne, 1973 (citation for a book).
McDonald, P., 'Youth Wages and Poverty', *Family Matters* no. 28, April 1991, pp. 28-31 (citation for an article in a journal).

For further information on referencing, especially on the increasingly-used Harvard system, consult Clanchy, J. and Ballard, B., *Essay Writing for Students: a practical guide*, Longman Cheshire, Melbourne, 1989, pp. 122-9.

# Presenting your research

It isn't easy to integrate your research material into your overall discussion. This is especially true with case studies and interviews where you have to relate the general to the particular. The most important observations should be woven into the main text, and you will have to present both your interpretation and illustrative material together. If you have too much detail for your text this can be placed in an appendix. For example, if you are interviewing an Aboriginal woman about her experience of white society, you would intersperse your general observations with evidence from your interview. If you felt the total interview should be included in your project, this could become an appendix.

Another approach is to separate the reporting of your research findings from your conclusions. A popular order for a report on survey research is:

Title page
Table of contents
List of tables
List of figures and photographs
Part 1: Presentation of aims (and research questions)
Part 2: Research methods (describing what you did and why you
    approached it this way)
Part 3: Statement of findings (which is the body of your project,
    where you record the results of your investigations)
Part 4: Conclusions
Endnotes
Bibliography
Appendixes

You should put a major part of your effort into the presentation of your research project. Depending on the nature and scope of your project, presenting the findings may be undertaken in a number of ways:

- written,
- visual,
- audio,
- video,

or combinations of more than one of these methods. Our advice has mostly been confined to written presentations, but taped, video and slide material can be incorporated into your research project presentations where appropriate.

A well-presented and well-arranged research project always assists the reader or assessor to understand the purpose and significance of your work. In the end, assessment of your project will rest on the quality of the work you have done and the quality of your analysis, also the extent to which you have been a responsible researcher. Can you honestly answer these questions?

- Is this project all your own work and not that of your parents, teachers or friends?
- Have you given sources for all the quotations you have used from other people's work?
- Have you stated who has lent you photographs or objects?
- Have you preserved confidentiality when it has been requested?
- Have you acknowledged help you have been given?

Now that you have checked your project you are ready to submit it confident that you have completed a thorough piece of work of which you can be proud, knowing that your work may be of value to future Australian researchers.

# 5

# ANNOTATED BIBLIOGRAPHY

## General reference - Australian studies

*APAIS, Australian Public Affairs Information Service: subject index to current literature.* Canberra 1957 -   .
Cumulative index issued monthly which includes current articles on Australian society, political, economic, social and cultural aspects. A valuable reference volume.

Appleton, R. & Appleton, B. *Dictionary of Australian Places.* Cambridge University Press, Melbourne 1992.
This listing gives population, climatic, and physical data for places in Australia. A quick reference to help understand any place in Australia.

*Australian Encyclopaedia.* The Grolier Society of Australia Pty. Ltd., Sydney 1983. 12 volumes.
Comprehensive reference work on all aspects of Australian society. Includes entries on significant individuals, events, places and subjects relating to Australian life. Also includes a detailed index and appendix in Volume 12. Excellent first resource.

Borchardt, D. H. (ed.) *Australians: a guide to sources.* Fairfax, Syme and Weldon Associates, NSW 1987.
A comprehensive guide to researching Australia from a historical perspective. It contains bibliographical information on works up to 1984 and is divided into categories which include Aborigines, Social History, and Labour.

Borchardt, D. H. *Checklist of Royal Commission and Select Committees of Parliament and Boards.* LaTrobe University, Bundoora 1986.
Collection of entries giving details from Commonwealth and states' enquiries 1960-1980. A very useful reference.

Duncan, J. S. *Atlas of Victoria.* Victorian Government Printing Office, Melbourne 1982.
Volume of maps with supporting text and photographs. Contains histori-

cal, geographical, social and cultural information relating to Victoria. A very good general resource.

Graetz, B., McAllister, I. *Dimensions of Australian Society.* Macmillan Co. of Australia Pty. Ltd., Melbourne 1988.
Good general guide to studies in Australian society covering areas such as ethnicity, gender, religion, class and politics. It has a comprehensive bibliography.

James, Walter (ed.) *Australian Studies: a survey.* Oxford University Press, Melbourne 1989.
A good reference work with an extensive bibliography.

Johnson, Ken *The AUSMAP Atlas of Australia.* Cambridge University Press, Melbourne 1992.
This atlas, compiled by the Australian Government Mapping Service, provides a wealth of information on the human resources of Australia, especially from the spatial and historical perspectives.

*Melbourne . . . A Social Atlas.* Commonwealth of Australia 1984. This volume is part of a series on all cities of Australia, and includes text and graphic information on demography, ethnicity, socio-economic factors and dwellings relating specifically to the metropolis.

## Surveys

Australian Bureau of Statistics *Australia — Working it out! Core material for Australian Studies.* AGPS, Canberra 1990.
Useful reference book for statistical data on Australian society. Graphic representation of data and useful information on using survey material.

Australian Bureau of Statistics *An introduction to sample surveys: a users' guide.* AGPS, Canberra 1988.
A useful book giving details of how surveys are used in research.

Castles, I. *Catalogue of Publications and Products 1990.* Australian Bureau of Statistics, Canberra 1990.
Essential guide to ABS publications and statistics. There are several reference indexes listed by subject, title and state.

Vamplew, W. (ed.) *Australians: historical statistics.* Fairfax, Syme & Weldon, Sydney 1987.
Collection of statistical information on Australian society from 1788. Contains demographic, economic, environmental, political and other

social data in the form of tables and graphics with accompanying text. A rich resource.

## Interviews

Douglas, L., Roberts. A., Thompson, R. *Oral History: a handbook.* Allen & Unwin, North Sydney 1988.
Good practical guide to conducting interviews and processing the data. It includes copyright information and technical expertise as well as good interviewing practices.

Kyle, Noeline *We Should've Listened to Grandma: women and family history.* Allen & Unwin, North Sydney 1988.
A useful, practical book about writing women into history through family research. It contains useful avenues for sources of information about women in Australian society.

Unger, M. *Voices from the Snowy.* NSW University Press 1989.
Collection of oral history interviews tracing the experiences of those who contributed to the Snowy River scheme. It combines photographs and text in a useful and informative way to tell the stories.

## Multicultural

Birtley, M. M., McQueen, P. *New Responsibilities: documenting multicultural Australia.* Museums Association of Australia and the Library Council of Victoria 1989.
A useful resource book about current issues relating specifically to many different ethnic groups in Australia.

Jupp, J. (ed.) *The Australian People: an encyclopaedia of the nation, its people and their origins.* Angus & Robertson, Sydney 1988.
A valuable source of information on the diversity of Australia as a multicultural society. Gives details of most ethnic groups and immigration patterns since white settlement.

## Historical

Alpin, Graeme, et al. (eds) *Australians: events and places.* Fairfax, Syme & Weldon, Sydney 1987.
This is complementary to the volume by Jupp, giving a chronological emphasis to history, and a geographical focus in the state-by-state accounts. Also a useful work.

Alpin, Graeme, et al. (eds) *Australians: a historical dictionary.* Fairfax, Syme & Weldon, Sydney 1987.
An alphabetic guide to Australian history; the entries are wide-ranging and include all major historical events and people. The biographical entries contain much useful information.

MacKinolty, Judy *Past Continuous: learning through historical environment.* History Teachers' Association, NSW 1983.
This volume was produced to develop research skills through historical projects. A useful source of project ideas.

Ritchie, J. (ed.) *Australian Dictionary of Biography.* Melbourne University Press, 1969-  .
These volumes include entries on prominent Australian people through the period 1788-1939. An essential reference about individuals in Australian history.

# Community

Project School Industry *A Student Guide to Doing Research Work in the Community: a handbook to help students get the most out of contacts with the community.* Ministry of Education and Training, Department of Labour and Industry. Victoria 1991.
This students guide is a handbook designed to help you get the most out of your community. It contains useful and practical material about contacting members of your own community for use as a research resource. It includes preparation, letter-writing, appointments, interviews, research methods and using library resources.

# Research presentation

Bate, D., Sharpe, P. *Student Writers' Handbook.* Harcourt Brace Jovanovich, Sydney 1990.
Handy book with help on reference books, library sources and general good advice for students.

Clanchy, J., Ballard, B. *Essay Writing for Students: a practical guide.* Longman Cheshire, Melbourne 1989.
A good practical book to help with essay writing in the arts and social sciences. It includes sections on essay topics, planning, drafting, referencing, editing and assessment. It gives practical advice on tackling essays under examination conditions.

Lane, Nancy D. *Techniques for Student Research: a practical guide.* Longman Cheshire, Melbourne 1989.
A useful book for students on the techniques of finding information, for example, using catalogues and indexes. Very comprehensive.

Wadsworth, Roland *Do It Yourself Social Research.* VCOSS/Allen & Unwin, Sydney 1989.
This book is aimed at community groups but contains some useful advice and information that could be of use to students as well.

## Media

*The Age.* Special feature 'The Media: a special report on ownership and control'. Melbourne 5 August 1991.

*Australian Government Publications.* AGPS, Canberra.
These volumes are cumulative indexes of all books, pamphlets and reports published by Commonwealth and state governments for any particular year.

Gordon, Harry *An Eye Witness History of Australia.* Penguin, Ringwood 1988.
This book explores Australian history through the eyes of the journalist. It contains contemporary accounts of events and people in chronological order and is a good source of material.

King, Jonathan *Stop Laughing, This is Serious: a social history of Australia in cartoons.* Cassell, Sydney 1978.
This is a chronological look at Australian history through the pictorial presentation of cartoons with an accompanying commentary. The *Bulletin* and *Punch* are major contributors.

Stewart, Donald E. *The Television Family: a content analysis of the portrayal of family life in prime time television.* Australian Institute of Family Studies, Melbourne 1983.
The report of a major study undertaken by the Institute of Family Studies of television and its role as interpreter of Australian society. It contains useful ideas about the analysis of media content.

## Ethnography

Bate, W. *Having a Go: Bill Boyd's Mallee.* Museum of Victoria, Melbourne 1989.
History through photos. Weston Bate has constructed the text of Mallee

history around the photography collection of Bill Boyd. A rich resource of historical visual material.

Bell, D. *Generations: grandmothers, mothers and daughters.* McPhee Gribble, Melbourne 1988.
Oral history woven into stories of generations of women. Photographs of artefacts are also used to tell the story of these generations of women.

Frost, L. *Dating Family Photos 1850-1920.* L. Frost, Essendon, Victoria 1990.
This book contains details to assist identification of 19th and 20th century photographs. It explains how to put them into their correct historical context.

# 6

# GLOSSARY OF TERMS

*abstract* — a summary of an article or a brief synopsis of a book.

*analysis* — the process of examining minutely; a study of the nature, functions and effects of something; a detailed description and criticism of something.

*annotated* — explanatory notes or extra information given, e.g. about a book in a bibliography.

*anthropology* — the study of people, their social organisation and cultural systems.

*appendix* — subsidiary material added at the end of a book.

*archives* — a place where historical records and documents are kept; documents thus preserved.

*artefact* — anything made by human workmanship.

*assessment* — the determination of the amount or value of something.

*atlas* — a volume of maps.

*bibliography* — a list of books relating to a particular author or subject.

*call number* — the classification number shown in the catalogue and on the cover of each book in a library. It is the book's address on the shelves and guides you to its location.

*catalogue* — a classified list. A library catalogue is a listing of books and other items. The classification system involves author, subject and title, with call numbers to identify specific items in an ordered system.

*CD–ROM* — 'Compact Disc – Read Only Memory'; a high-density means of storing information for access by computer. Some libraries store a variety of information by this means.

*classification* — the arrangement of things according to certain categories.

*community* — a society of people linked together by common conditions of life, beliefs, etc., or organised under one authority.

*copyright* — the exclusive right of an author, artist, etc., to reproduce his or her own works during a certain period fixed by law.

*cross-analysis* — the comparison of data or information by the examination of relationships between different sections of data.

*data* — a group of known, given or ascertained facts, from which inferences or a conclusion can be drawn.

*deduction* — coming to a conclusion about something, based on it following a certain general rule.

*demographic* — to do with the study of a population, particularly the birth, death, health and general living conditions of the people.

*demonstrate* — to explain or prove by reasoning, evidence or experiment; to show the working of.

*encyclopaedia* — a book or set of books of classified information on all branches of knowledge, or on one specified branch, usually arranged alphabetically.

*ethnography* — can also be called participant observation. It is the study of people in groups by being part of the group and using set techniques to analyse the social characteristics of the group.

*footnote* — an explanatory note inserted at the foot of the page (or an *endnote* if it is at the end of a chapter or book).

*hypothesis* — an unproven theory; a provisional explanation of observed facts.

*index* — an alphabetical list of names or subjects in a book, with page references.

*Local Government Area (LGA)* — an area governed by a shire council, or municipality of some kind, referred to in some statistics about different places.

*material culture* — objects that people use in their every-day life, which form some of the physical forms of the culture of the society at that time.

*mean* — the average of two or more values. Add the values together, then divide the result by the number of values you started with.

*media* — a collective term for communication, including newspapers, TV and radio.

*median* — the value of a quantity so that exactly half of a particular population have greater values than that quantity.

*microform* — books, journals and documents kept on microfilm and microfiche. These are reduced photographic images on rolls or sheets of film; these are loaded into machines which project an image onto a screen, so the pages can be viewed and read separately.

*mode* — the statistical category having the most examples in it.

*oral history* — history recorded from the spoken word through interviews.

*periodical* — a magazine or journal published at regular intervals of more than one day.

*plagiarism* — the wrongful attempt to pass off another's work as one's own, without permission or acknowledgement. It is a form of cheating.

*primary source* — the original research, such as first-hand information, such as interviews, surveys or statistics.

*random* — occurring without a particular plan or purpose.

*reference* — an indication of the source of a quotation, or some extra information.

*reference book* — a book meant to be consulted for specific information.

*representative* — typical of a group or class of things; containing examples of many types.

*research* — scholarly investigation and study aiming at adding to the sum of knowledge on some specific subject.

*sampling frame* — the total number of people (for example) for whom the survey is relevant, of whom some will be selected to be surveyed or interviewed.

*secondary source* — information which has already been gathered in another form, for example, a book or other publication.

*speculation* — forming an opinion about something without having a great deal of information about it.

*statistics* — numerical data relevant to any problem or study.

*stratified* — arranged in groups, usually of increasing or decreasing status.

*stratified sample* — a sample number of a larger group which closely reflects some particular characteristic of the larger group.

*study* — to apply one's mind to learning, especially from books; to learn systematically; to analyse or examine carefully.

*survey* — to take a general view of; to look at as a whole; to examine the condition and value of; to inspect and assess.

*synopsis* — an abstract; a brief summary of an article or book.

*systematic* — methodical according to a specific order or plan.

*word processing* — a computer-based process for producing documents.

# 7

# INDEX

**A**

abstracts  28-9
academic books  30-1
APAIS  29
analysis of results  66-8, 88-90, 105
anthropology  86, 90
appendix  106-7
archives  20
artefacts  97-101
    data sheet  99
assessment  105-6
atlases  29
audio-visual material  22-4
Australian Bureau of
        Statistics  33-4

**B**

bibliography  28, 30, 107
books
    academic  30-1
    how to find  25-7
    how to use  27-34
    reference  22, 27-9
buildings  90-6

**C**

call number  26
catalogue  25-7
CD-ROM  70-1
classification of books  25-6
community resources  50-5

how to contact  52-5
computer
    hardware  66, 68-71
    software  68-71
content analysis  40-4, 48-9
cross-analysis  67

**D**

data presentation  32-4, 70
database software  70
demography  29
Dewey system  25-6
dictionaries  28

**E**

electoral resources  32-3
electronic media
        *see* television *and* radio
encyclopaedias  27-8
ethnography  86-90

**F**

family history  101-2
footnotes  31, 107

**G**

government publications  32
graphs  34-5

**H**

house plans 91
hypothesis 12

**I**

index 28-9, 30
informant profile 74, 76-8
information
  networks 70-1
  sources of 15-17, 27-39, 50-2
interviews 71-85
  analysis 84-5
  group 81-3
  informant profile 76-8
  preparation 74-9
  questions 79-81
  record of 74-5
  reliability 73-4
  steps 71
  summary 83-4
  transcription of 83-4
  validity 84
  who? 72-9
  why? 71-2

**L**

letter-writing 53-5
library 19-34
  catalogue 25-7
  plan 21
  types 20
  using 19-27

**M**

maps 29
material culture 90-104
  artefacts 97-100
  buildings 90-6
  built environment 95-6, 102-4
  interpretation 100-1

streetscapes 93-5
mean 34, 67
media 34-50
median 34, 67
microform 22-4
  microfiche 23-4
  microfilm 23-4
mode 34, 67
multicultural Australia 66, 104

**N**

newspapers 34-44
  compiling collection 39
  content analysis 40-5
  index of newsclippings
    collection 39-40
  research tool 36-9
  storage 39-40
  types 36

**O**

opinion polls 33
oral history 71-85
  importance 85
  interpretation 100-1

**P**

participant observation 86-90
  access 87
  analysis 88-90
  evaluation sheet 89
  problems 86-7
  recording 87-9
  research steps 87-90
periodicals 22, 31-2
personal contact 52-5
photocopying 25
photographs 101-4
  pictorial data sheet 103
plagiarism 107
presentation 105-9

**Q**

questions  60-4
questionnaire  64
    *see also* survey

**R**

radio  49-50
reading
    general  27-9
    specific  30-4
recording responses  66, 87-8
references  106-7
reference book  22, 27-9
research project
    analysis  105
    assessment  105-6
    checklist  106
    choice of  12-13
    methods  17
    order of items in report  108
    planning  11-17
    presentation  105-9
    questions  12-15
    references for  106-7
    skills  57, 59
    strategy  17
    topic  12, 13
resources, existing  19-55
        *see also* Australian Bureau of
        Statistics, books, library,
        newspapers periodicals,
        radio, television

**S**

sampling techniques  65-6

statistics  32-4
    ABS, how to use  33-4
stratified sample  65-6
streetscapes  93-6
street surveys
    data collection forms  94, 96
survey  58-68
    conducting  64-6
    five steps  58-68
        *see also* questionnaire

**T**

tape recording  75, 79-81
telephone calls  52-4
television  44-9
    advertising  48
    content analysis  48-9
    current affairs  47
    film & drama  47-8
    news  46-7
    sport  48
translating questionnaires  66

**V**

video cassette collection  23
visual resources  90-104
    photographs  93, 101-2, 103
        *see also* buildings, streetscapes

**W**

word processing  70

**Y**

yearbooks  28

Grateful acknowledgement is made to the following for their assistance in both providing suitable material and granting Cambridge University Press permission to reproduce it in this text:

Deakin University Library and Media Unit; *The Australian*; Australian Bureau of Statistics; Allen & Unwin, Sydney, for the 'Informant Profile' from Douglas, Roberts and Thompson's *Oral History: A Handbook* (1988); A V Jennings Homes.

Every effort has been made to trace and acknowledge copyright but in some cases this has not been possible. Cambridge University Press would welcome any information that would redress this situation.